Generations

GENERATIONS
A HISTORICAL METHOD

by
Julián Marías

translated by
HAROLD C. RALEY

THE UNIVERSITY OF ALABAMA PRESS
University, Alabama

Translated into English from *El metodo histórico de las generaciones*
Copyright © 1967 by Julián Marías
English translation and addenda copyright © 1970
by THE UNIVERSITY OF ALABAMA PRESS
Library of Congress Catalog Card Number: 70–121041
Standard Book Number: 8173–6611–3
Manufactured in the United States of America

Table of Contents

Translator's Preface

PHILOSOPHER, SOCIAL SCIENTIST, literary critic, translator, teacher, writer, public speaker—Julián Marías is not readily characterized in terms of a single occupational description. His life and his method transcend the arbitrary limits of the conventional academic disciplines and subdisciplines, many of which are seemingly becoming even narrower in scope the more obvious man's need becomes for the kind of comprehensive approach that distinguishes Marías' writings. The present work on the concept of generations is a fine example of such comprehensiveness, in that it contributes to the disciplines of history, sociology, and philosophy with almost equal meaning and promise.

Marías' versatility might lead some to assume that his contributions to particular disciplines, considered separately, are superficial or even cavalier. Nothing could be further from the truth. This is not to suggest that his mastery of various disciplines, though undeniably impressive, is total in every case. Rather one might say, at the risk of oversimplification, that his uniqueness is less the result of a conventional mastery of many fields than it is the reflection of a basic philosophical perspective that informs all of his works and enables him to discern previously unsuspected meanings in any topic he considers, however familiar or even hackneyed it may be. His *Historia de la filosofía,* now in its twenty-fourth printing and widely hailed for its remarkably fresh and fertile approach to the history of philosophical ideas, is an excellent case in point.

Several captions suggest themselves, as one seeks to characterize Marías' philosophical and intellectual orientation. First of all, he is an "Ortegan" philosopher in the sense that he accepts José Ortega y Gasset's basic tenets of "radical reality," "circumstance," "vital reason," and, of course, "generations." But to say that he is Ortegan is not to imply that he merely echoes or enlarges on Ortega's thought. Indeed, the very nature of the Ortegan philosophy as such precludes any mere discipleship or static scholasticism. Unlike most philosophies, which are strangely indifferent to temporality (or seek to be), Ortegan thought is profoundly committed to a passionate concern for the future. As both Marías and Ortega have pointed out, theirs is not a closed system conceived in and limited to a certain time and place, but rather an open-ended enterprise—an invitation for others to join them in an unfinished, and perhaps never to be finished, task of great importance.

Moreover, it has not been adequately recognized by students of Ortega's philosophy that some of the fundamental notions of the mode of thought attributed to him—and rightly so—perhaps belong equally to Marías, Ortega's friend and collaborator for many years. For instance, Ortega's sociological theories were not published until 1957, in *El hombre y la gente* [Man and People], two years after his death in 1955, and two years after Marías' publication of *his* definitive "Ortegan" work on the same matters, *La estructura social* [The Social Structure]. As for the problem of generations, Ortega never considered the concept formally in a single work. In fact—I say this with all due regard for his truly awesome importance in Spanish letters and thought—Ortega never wrote a book—at least not a complete book—on *any* single subject. Thus it remained for Marías to formulate a mature "Ortegan" concept of generations, and while one senses the importance of this concept in much of Ortega's work, it is only by way of Marías' treatment that the concept becomes clear. Much is made of the influence of the older generations on the younger, but the effect of the young on the old is also a very real, though all too often ignored, phenomenon—as the collaborative relationship of Ortega and Marías demonstrates.

Generally speaking, there are two opposing schools of thought concerning the origins and importance of the philosophical movement of which Marías is the most brilliant living proponent and exegete. On the one hand, there are those who trace its origins through Ortega to Germany and explain it away as a belated offshoot of a tradition going back to Nietzsche and Kant. On the other hand, there are fervent defenders who see in this "Ortegan" philosophy an utterly new and unique view of reality. A brief translator's preface is not the appropriate forum in which to attempt to settle this question, which has been argued, often quite heatedly, for more than fifty years. Even so, it is interesting to note that both Ortega and Marías—and we could add Unamuno—are guided by the same spirit that led Plato to philosophize. All these thinkers realized that both the first and the final problems of philosophy belong not to philosophers but simply to men, and that men philosophize, in the final analysis, not merely because they are capable of doing so but because they *must* do so.

It is here, I believe, that we find the real key to Marías' versatility. He does not pursue problems back and forth across the boundaries of the arts and the academic disciplines as a matter of

x

whim. Rather, he considers the complex problems of men in real life, as distinct from the artifically simplified problems of the schoolroom. Academic problems are neatly defined, man's problems are not, and the latter must be followed whereever they lead—if not to a solution, at least to their conclusion. Marías has been described as "Ortegan," implying although not explaining the rich heritage of this mode of thought. But mere adherence to a mode of thought is idle unless it arises from a deeper commitment. To put it another way: Ortega represents a starting point for Marías, but this fact alone tells us little or nothing of Marías' final aims or of his worth as a philosopher. Any legacy, philosophical or otherwise, may be squandered if the heir is not up to meeting the responsibility imposed on him.

This brings us to another caption that might well be considered as the very woof in the fabric of Marías' thought. In a phrase heavy with meanings, Marías describes philosophy as *"la visión responsable,"* as responsible vision. This is far from being applicable to much that currently goes under the name of philosophy, sad to say, but it does apply, and most readily, to Marías' thought. There is no need to go into detail concerning all of the deeper meanings implied by the phrase, except to say that the word "responsible" is to be taken in its most literal and moral sense. Philosophy, in Marías' view, "responds" to the problems, realities, and possibilities of man *in the real world*. It is a grave "responsibility" indeed, for the philosopher committed to be true to his task must always seek to understand and explain the human condition, and in so doing, he assumes willy nilly the duty of enabling men to survive their most serious failures—and their successes.

Marías has made such a commitment. With courage and clarity, imbued with deep sympathies and an abiding respect for the extraordinary multiplicity of human possibilities, he has con-

sidered the grave and subtle problems of our time. And he has
done so without becoming insensitive to life's tenderest and most
poetic manifestations. If occasionally he has erred, as he seems
to have done, for example, in the closing pages of the present
work, when he suggests that the turbulence of the years between
1931 and 1946 will be followed by a period of relative calm,
he has done so out of his deep concern for life's fullest possibilities. This is not to imply that his work is tainted by any wishful
thinking or utopianism. For Marías, the real world is more
promising by far than any imagined realm could ever be. In any
case, his passion for the truth always outweighs any fear of falling into error in the pursuit of it.

This brings us once again to the question of Marías' varied
interests and the multiplicity of themes encountered in his work.
These interests are bound together by a moral commitment to
the total human condition ("nothing human is alien to him").
This moral unity "corresponds" to another unity, another system,
which arises from the fundamental structure of human life.
Marías does not impose system on the reality he treats; instead,
he discovers system within that reality. The reality of the generations is essential to that system and cannot really be considered
apart from the totality it implies. But of this I need say no more,
for in a sense it is the theme of the present work.

Stillwater, Oklahoma   Harold C. Raley
September 1970

Generations

1

The Generations Theme

THE GENERATIONS THEME MAY BE CONSIDERED EITHER quite old or quite new, depending on one's point of view. The fact of "generations" has been a part of human experience for thousands of years. Yet systematic study of the subject is a comparatively recent development, so much so that it is only now beginning to be considered with scientific rigor.

The concept of the generations appears often in the literature of the Semitic world. We recall, for example, the many references in the Old Testament to punishments reaching "unto the fourth generation." In the New Testament an even more explicit mention is made when Saint Matthew, at the beginning of his gospel, sets forth the genealogy of Jesus Christ: "The book of the generation of Jesus Christ, the son of David, the son of Abraham. Abraham begat Isaac; and Isaac begat Jacob; and Jacob begat Judas and his brethren; and Judas begat Phares and Zara of Thamar. . . ." And he concludes: "So all the generations from Abraham to David are fourteen generations; and from David until the carrying away into Babylon are fourteen generations; and from the carrying away into Babylon unto Christ are fourteen generations." [1] We see here the use of the generations concept, obviously conceived in a genealogical sense, as a measure of historical reality. In the same gospel we find the word *generation* being used by Jesus to designate those living in his time: "Verily I say unto you, This generation [*haec generatio, ἡ γενεὰ αὗτη*] shall not pass till all these things be fulfilled." [2] There are similar references in other places.

In the Hellenic world too, we find early references to the notion of generations. Homer sees human history as a succession of generations, and in a simile of imperishable beauty—though not without some risk of exaggeration—compares them to the leaves of the trees:

> As the leaves
> of the trees are born and perish,
> thus pass the ages of man:
> old leaves to earth are dashed
> by autumn winds; others nurtured
> by the flowering forest, proudly
> grow in Spring's living breath;
> and the generations of man are so:
> one is born and another passes away. [3]

Nestor, the Iliad tells us, had seen two generations of men die in Pilos and he reigned over a third. [4]

In Greece, the most important text in which the idea of generations appears is the well known work of Herodotus. He

1. Matthew 1:1–17.
2. Ibid., 24:34.
3. Iliad, 6, 146–49. The original Greek reads as follows:

   οἵη περ φύλλων γενεή, τοιήδε και ἀνδρῶν.
   φύλλα τὰ μέν τ᾽ ἄνεμος χαμάδις χέει, ἄλλα δέθ᾽ὕλη
   τηλεθόωσα φύει᾽ ἔαρος δ᾽ἐπιγίγνεται ὥρη᾽
   ὣς ἀνδρῶν γενεὴ ἡμὲν φύει, ἠδ᾽ἀπολήγει.

4. Ibid., 1, 250–252.

refers to the Egyptian use of the generation as the basic unit of historical chronology and determines with complete—perhaps excessive—accuracy the span of history and the exact number of past generations: "The Egyptians and their priests told me, and their monuments verified it, that counting from the first king until the priest of Vulcan, the last to reign there, three hundred and forty-one generations had lived in that period, and during that span in Egypt there had been a similar succession of high priests and an equal number of kings. Counting a hundred years for each three generations, the three hundred mentioned come to a sum of ten thousand years, and the remaining forty-one total eleven thousand three hundred and forty."[5]

This genealogical understanding of the duration of a generation as the mean distance between parents and children is, with slight modifications, generally accepted in Greece. For Hecataeus of Miletus, a generation lasts forty years, for Hellanicus, only thirty. Ephorus holds with the calculations of Herodotus. Figures of this magnitude are repeated whenever the duration of a generation is interpreted from the physical point of view—in terms, that is, of genealogy. They will not be changed until the generation is understood in terms of completely different postulates.

The Scientific Problem

The idea of the generations, despite its long history in the accumulation of life experience, has had a very brief existence as a scientific problem. The earliest attempts to elaborate facts about generations and to convert them into knowledge date from only about a century ago. From that time until the early years of

5. Herodotus, 2, 142. The key phrase is the chronological definition of the generation:

γενεαὶ γὰρ τρεῖς ἀνδρῶν ἑκατὸν ἔτεά ἐστι.

the twentieth century, we find only scattered and uncertain attempts in the struggle to master the elusive and difficult reality of the generations. The more penetrating and coherent efforts have been concentrated in the last thirty years.[6] Why should this be so? Is it that perhaps for the first time in history men have come to feel an urgent need to know just what a generation is and to what generation they themselves belong?

Recall how the characters and stage setting of a play were described, until quite recently, in the traditional theater program: "Don Pedro," we read, "fifty years old; Elvira, his daughter, twenty years old." Then, below the list of *dramatis personae,* we find: "Present time"—a vague qualification indeed. What did it mean? "This time" is generally taken to mean a little more than a century, that is, almost all of the nineteenth century and a few decades of the twentieth or, to put it another way, little more than the time elapsed since wigs and frock coats went out of style. However, neither audience, actors, nor directors were unduly concerned. In the vague sense in which history books speak of the "contemporary period," "contemporary" works used to be staged, almost without exception, with current dress and hair styles. This may seem less surprising if we remember that such works were experienced by audiences as immediate events. We can recall having seen the girls in a performance of *La verbena de la Paloma*[7] costumed in the latest dress and hair styles. Nowadays, however, all this has changed completely, and no one would dare forget that *La verbena* dates from 1894; neither could the details of staging that place it in that year be omitted

6. Written in 1949 [translator's note].
7. A popular late-nineteenth century *zarzuela,* or Spanish operetta. The title refers to a festival (*verbena*) "of the Dove" in Madrid [translator's note].

by the producer. Why is this so? Is it because those who go to the theater these days are more sophisticated than theatergoers used to be? Whatever the reason, we find that indifference to chronological detail would reduce audience enjoyment considerably, and that the spectators would be disturbed by temporal anachronisms.

What this means is that the reality of that time—1894—has faded away. In the short span of our lifetime, which finds some of us still quite young, a new situation has come into being. Rarely has history revealed anything comparable. History always implies an essential element of novelty, but a curious "historical modesty" makes it difficult for us to believe that something truly new and unprecedented has arisen before our eyes. This situation, which of late has arisen, is usually called "historical awareness."[8] One of the most disturbing consequences of this proclivity is that every proper name must be bounded by two dates. When we say "Cervantes (1547–1616)" we are serene and sure of ourselves. But what of our own lives? They are bordered by only one date, and this seems to imply a strange imperfection. Yet in fact, to be alive is to be precisely this: imperfect, unperfected, unfinished, inconclusive. The question mark that stands for the as yet undetermined date of our death—1914–?—underlines the problematic and disquieting character of human life when its precise temporal setting is unknown. We cannot understand the meaning of what a man says unless we know *when* he said it and *when* he lived. Until quite recently, one could read a book or contemplate a painting without knowing the exact period during which it was brought into being. Many such works were held up as "timeless" models beyond all chronological servitude. Today,

8. See Julián Marías, *Introducción a la Filosofía* (Madrid, 1947), p. 33; this work is included in volume 2 of Marías, *Obras*, 7 vols. (Madrid, 1961–68), pp. 1–367.

however, all undated reality seems vague and invalid, having the insubstantial form of a ghost. As we stroll through the streets of a city we see not only a present reality but also the heritage of successive generations of men who, by their living, have created the reality. At the same time we also imagine and anticipate the future: within ten years, we think, this street will be narrow, that garden will be replaced by a building. Facing any human reality —an ideology, an artistic tendency, a social custom, a political regime—we ask ourselves automatically: when will it end?, how long will it last? It is not that we wish to see something troublesome disappear, for the question applies quite as readily to our likes as it does to our dislikes. And in either case the question is complete only when we add another to it: when did it begin?

The reasons for this bent or state of mind are complex and we will not enter here into a detailed analysis of them all. Two are sufficient to guide us at this point. The first is contemporary man's mental awareness of a long historical past. The second is a progressive quickening of the historical rhythm, an acceleration in the tempo of history. One of the causes of this acceleration, one that I have stressed in previous writings, is the enormous increase in the number of positive and negative "impacts" being received by man. These may be things that happened *before* and are now merely important to a man, or they may be things that happen *to* him. Until recently, owing to slow and scant communications, only the most immediate events could really matter to a person. News of far-off happenings either did not reach him or, if it did, seemed meaningless and "lifeless" because of the delay. Only a small number of events in any area affected and influenced the individual powerfully enough to leave in their wake a discernible variation in his life. We must not think only of remote times. In Revolutionary Paris the most violent disturbances could occur in one part of the city while people in other parts knew nothing of them. At best, news of what had happened was tardy and vague.[9] Today, as everyone knows, we are notified of the most distant happenings, in great profusion and in ways that make these events seem very immediate: the modern communications media enable us to be present, almost, at events throughout the world. As a result, our life seems assailed by a ceaseless rush of waves.

Yet this is not all. For some time now, we of the West have been becoming increasingly aware of the fleeting, quickening pace of historical life, and this very "awareness" now functions as a new ingredient in our life and thus has become an additional factor in its acceleration. There is a difference between the actual acceleration of the historical tempo and men's knowing about it, just as there is between one's having a disease and knowing that one has it. It is no longer merely a question of considering an impression passively; it is a question of being alert to a change already foreseen and counted on—of anticipating the change. In considering the spectacle of life, an optical change has come

9. Cf. Jean Robiquet, *La vie quotidienne au temps de la Révolution* (Paris, 1938), p. 98: "We have just seen how the different districts of Paris were separated from one another, and how slowly news spread in them. . . . Never was this more apparent than during the September massacres. The *'tape-dur'* [executioners] could assemble a hundred wretches in the Court of la Conciergerie without attracting the attention of passers-by on la Barillerie Street or on the Court du Mail. Even the tragedies at Carmes did not break the silence. Neither the inhabitants of Regard Street, nor the three hundred armed bourgeois who were training in the Luxembourg Gardens, nor the customers at the refreshment bar under the trees in the garden, had the slightest idea of what was happening. For all they knew about it, they could have been living at Compiègne or Orléans. And when the matter became known, there was little emotion and that far from being widespread." [Unless otherwise stated, this and subsequent citations not translated in the body of the text have been set into English by the translator (translator's note).]

about: the "simple view" has been replaced by Marcel Proust's myopic eye. In certain recent films—especially English but also those of the other European and American countries (it is a widespread phenomenon and thus is all the more interesting)—the lives of people who are still living are reconstructed. A careful time technique is applied to that reconstruction: furniture, dress, hairdos, music, and expressions of speech are scrupulously selected with a view to the date. One will hear a certain tango because the year is 1921; skirts of a certain length will be seen because it is now 1939; an adjective will be used that became popular in 1927 and went out of style two years later.[10] We feel, not without a certain anguish probably unknown to men before us, that archaeology is being made of our very lives. And at the same time we feel that as we make this optical change, we must also replace the calculations based on an intelligent view with others from a more exact source. What will this source be? The mathematician? No, it will be another even more exact: the historian. If this choice appears surprising it is because historians are still not so good at history as some mathematicians are at mathematics.

The present, then, is vanishing. It is shrinking to a tenuous thread, to an instant. What does *today* mean? We do not know; perhaps it means only this December 14—the barren "today" of the calendar. There is no firm ground underfoot. Man feels that he is floating in a fast-flowing current. What is there to cling to? Whatever the possible advantages of this distressing situation, there is none in remaining in it—yet there seems to be no escape. It is useless even to try to return to firm ground, for here we are, willy nilly, trying to stay afloat in midstream. There is no escaping our history. And because this situation is no mere theory but

10. As an especially clear example, I remember a film entitled *The Courtney Household,* which is confined to the years elapsed in this century.

a form of human life, it is idle to be overly disturbed by it. Even should we, for example, "reject" the situation, we are, like it or not, no less a part of it. For history is something that happens *today* to us all. We can only accept the fact and try to discover some reason for it. This is the truly human recourse, and because of it we have come to see in recent years that "reason" must be *historical* reason.

However, the way of history must not be confused with the "historicism" that has been so widely discussed in recent years. Historicism is not a situation but a theory and it is, therefore, problematic and debatable. Is it a good theory? It may be an error, not because it removes the firm footing of happier times —no theory could—but rather because in the final analysis it is unfaithful to history: in short, because it is lacking in historicity.[11]

We must seek the present, "the now," that eludes us. In referring to the present, we often say "these days" or "our time." But just whose time do we mean? When an old man says "in my day" he is referring not the present in which he actually lives and speaks but to some past time. Although he lives today, it is apparent that this is not "his" time. To which portion of the past does he feel he belongs? With what zone of his life does it coincide? When an old person speaks of "my time," meaning some past period, he seems to reveal that he lives in the present as an exile or an alien. Are not our lives formed by the very subtle essence of a certain period?

The Ages of Man

This presumed bond of man to just a certain portion of the total time allotted to him as a living being leads us to the theme of "human ages." In considering this theme one tends to think,

11. Cf. Julián Marías, *Introducción* . . . , chapter 3, "Verdad e Historia" [Truth and History].

first of all, of the biological factor: growth, full development, aging, and finally death of the organism. Biology surely has much to do with the problem of the several human ages and yet, for reasons that will become clearly evident later, biology is not the major and certainly not the decisive factor. Human ages are also historical ages and as such they are affected by an essential variation that alters their duration and character from one era to another. The pattern changes from time to time and is first apparent in speech. Linguistic usages are old by their very nature. They retain traces of previous situations. Hence the linguistically sound expression "an elderly man of sixty" clashes with the realities of our day. It still *sounds* good enough, but by today's standards a man of sixty is by no means "old." On the other hand, the expression "a girl of thirty-five" sounds a bit odd linguistically. And yet in fact we consider the majority of women of that age "girls" and often call them that.

Compare this situation with another in which we find the other extreme. In the Romantic Era, not only do we find that a great number of the leading figures of the time die before the age of fifty—and a good many before thirty—but also that both men and women mature very early and reach their full standing at ages that most people today consider juvenile. Normally a certain longevity is essential in becoming "famous." Yet Mariano José de Larra—that man of the world, that prestigious writer, so disillusioned and blasé—died at twenty-eight! José de Espronceda, the "Spanish Byron," died at thirty-four, and Byron himself expired at thirty-six. Mariana Pineda, widowed with two children, was still not twenty-seven when she was hanged in 1831. Julia, the widowed countess *Imperiali* in Schiller's *Friesco,* is portrayed unmistakably as a woman in her autumn years: "A very tall and corpulent lady. A proud coquette. A beauty somewhat dissipated by excesses. Striking but not pleasant. Her face shows a malicious and mocking character." As for her age, however, we read: "Twenty-five."

This arouses in us a grave suspicion. Is it not a mistake to interpret generations in terms of biological age, when we notice in these generations a decisive historical component? The word *generation* alludes to the act of engendering and hence to "genealogy." The word has almost always been understood in this way, as we see, for example, in the passage quoted from Saint Matthew. This understanding accounts for the notion that the approximate duration of a generation is thirty years, since it is supposed that man fathers his children at about the age of thirty. Now, while this is quite clear up to a point in dealing with an isolated family, it becomes complicated when families are intermarried. To begin with, even in monogamous societies, children may be born ten, twenty, or thirty years apart. In polygamous groupings the age difference can well be as much as fifty years. The complexity increases still further in groups whose members live promiscuously without families in the strict sense: could it be that among such peoples there are no generations? On the other hand, is the world that the adolescent finds as he enters life really that of his parents? It often happens that he is influenced by teachers and writers who are much younger than his parents, midway between him and the parents, and who play a decisive and quite different role from that of the parents. This obliges us to state an all-important problem: the *"setting"* of generations. Over against genealogy, which is a feature of the family, it is evident that this setting is not of a familial order. Thus, we have to conclude that the setting of generations is society and thence history. And this brings us to a formal inquiry into the biographical and social structure of human ages.

Time that *passes* is one thing; the age that one *is* is another. As I have said elsewhere[12] "the child and the adolescent realize that living is doing things one after another with an aim to being finally 'grown up.' When they ask themselves what they are

12. Ibid., p. 77.

14

going to be, they feel headed toward a form of adult life which they see as endowed with substance and stability. While this happens, life . . . seems indefinite and limitless; one can be many things, anything, or 'everything.' This is why the life of a very young man or woman still has no *form*. Rather it is pure indetermination and possibility. However, as one begins to reach 'adulthood,' he realizes that this state does not mean remaining in a fixed present, but rather that to live is to keep on doing things in view of the future. The vital horizon, like the visual, withdraws as one advances toward it. And when the horizon begins to take on a precise contour, when one senses life's limits and sees it ending in death in the future, then life is lived as something finished, with a certain style and inner structure. It is as though one were living with his days numbered. The span of life is not pure quantity, but rather is qualitatively differentiated. It is not that we are given so much time; it is that this *quantum* is always a *quale*. The age structure diversifies time and makes each portion of it unique, not in the sense that each is irretrievable, but rather that none is interchangeable with another. There is an age to play with a hoop, another to be a student, and another to be a teacher; and unless one does these things at their due time, they will never be done."[13] Hence, life assumes a certain form and each temporal fragment has its precise place within it. At each moment, man finds himself at a certain "level" of life. The road taken and the vicissitudes experienced are retained in age, and this endows any instant of life with temporality. Age is the form that time takes to dwell within us.

Historical Life

Up to now we have considered only individual life, and yet when a man begins to live he soon discovers that human life preceded him and will continue after his death. This alien "life,"

13. Ibid., p. 72.

surrounding but not belonging to the individual, is called "historical" life. But a strange thing happens to the word *life* when an adjective such as *historical* is appended to it—a grave problem but one that cannot be treated here.[14] It is enough to say that history is also qualified time, although in another sense. There occurs something analogous to what we have just seen in the matter of human ages: times are historical not because they are mere duration or any time at random but because they have a certain distinguishing quality. Each period is a form of life among other forms, and each presupposes and needs the others. Just as the individual's age means a certain level of life, so each period is a certain level of time.

This carries with it the necessity of a plurality of men so that not only history but also the succession of human generations will be possible. The lives of men who succeed each other must partially overlap. If the contrary were true, each man, each group, would have to repeat the "Adamic" situation indefinitely. Partial coexistence and partial succession are therefore necessary, and they give meaning to the expression "historical coexistence." Now this does not refer to something added haphazardly or extrinsically to an individual life that would otherwise not be historical. The ingredients of which we make our lives, what we call "things" (the latter are, strictly speaking, human interpretations of reality, the result of what other men have experienced and done), are historical and hence, in an intrinsic and essential sense, life itself. Nevertheless, the attributes of individual life differ in a fundamental way from those of history.

Individual Life	*History*
Mine (that is, of each person).	Not only mine, but also and primarily that of others.

14. Ibid., p. 72.

An unfinished task ahead.	Not wholly unfinished, but partially completed already.
Something I have to do alone.	Not only I, nor I alone.
Radical solitude.	Radical coexistence.

We see to what extent these are differing realities. History is not life. Life is only what is truly individual; it is *my* life, what is given me, but given in an unfinished state. It is something that I must *do* at every instant of time, and in radical solitude. Yet it is also apparent, paradoxically, that if history is not life neither is it created from something other than "life." Here arises the grave problem of "historical" life, for despite its being a form of life, it is essentially incompatible with individual existence, which is to say with life in the full meaning of the term.

"I" am not the subject of history, nor is any individual man; nor does history deal with the plural subject composed of many individuals considered *as such*. The subject of history is society, which is a system of *usages*. This should not be taken to mean that history, which is so different from society in principle, is something that happens merely to society. Society does not move and direct itself; the old idea of a social statics and dynamics is especially erroneous and misleading, and the nucleus of truth that it attempted to express must be applied to a quite different scheme. Society is only society *historically*. This means that its very inner texture is from the beginning dynamic and historical, because its historicity lies in what is termed a "situation." As I have shown elsewhere, an absolute situation would be an absurdity. A "present" situation only becomes such when it is weighed against past experiences and especially against future aims. It would be absurd to define man's situation as that of a being trapped or imprisoned on the planet Earth. Yet should it occur to him to leave our globe and go to other planets, then his situation on earth really could become—appear to be—one of confinement or imprisonment.

Each situation is, then, a level of a certain movement. Better said—in terms that are more concrete and human, more metaphorical and hence more rigorously true—history is a drama with a plot and characters. And with this we return to the beginning: who are the characters, the "who" of historical life? What are their "ages"? What is the "unity of time," that present which had vanished before us? In other words, what is the elemental "present" of history? This, in summary, is the theme of this book.

2

The Problem of Generations
in the
Nineteenth Century

As a theme arising out of human experience at a rather elementary level, the idea of generations is one of the oldest of concepts; as a scientific theme, as a problem of historiology, it is one of the newest. Its modernity allows us to be present at its birth, and to trace its subsequent vicissitudes as an intellectual question. As such, it presents several odd characteristics, of which one of the oddest, surely, is the rather small number of thinkers to study it seriously and profoundly. Moreover, these few writers seem generally to have been quite unaware of each other's interest in the theme. As a rule, the problem has not been handed along from one man to another, and each has come to it by way of personal motivations peculiar to himself. This very fact makes their community of interest all the more striking, and imparts a certain air of familiarity and even of collaboration in their shared preoccupation with a problem of interest to so few.

Just who were these men, who felt this strange attraction to the generations theme? Looking back, it seems that one might have been able to predict in advance to which human "types" the generations theme would appeal, and therefore, the period in history during which scientific consideration of the theme would begin. We are dealing with two types of man: a) the first discoverers of the reality that is "human life," and b) certain gifted men who in the course of long and demanding political and statistical careers gained experience in the practical manipulation of generational data (birth and death dates, family histories, etc.). Both these human types appear in the early years of the nineteenth century, at a time when man had behind him a long historical past, scientifically elaborated, and was beginning to acquire an exact knowledge of European populations and their variations, and a time when philosophy, concurrently, was focusing for the first time on the problem of the peculiarity of human life and historical reality.

The isolated nature of the early efforts to arrive at a theory of generations and a general lack of knowledge about these efforts combine to make a history of the theme quite difficult. Indeed, such a history still remains to be written. I know of only five attempts in this direction—one in French, three in German, one in Spanish—and all of them are more or less fragmentary and generally very uneven in scope and worth. The earliest of these works, that of François Mentré,[1] is undoubtedly the most complete and informative, taking into account its date of publication (1920). The second, a very brief work, is an essay by Karl Mannheim.[2] The third, successful despite its manifest inferiority, is the well-known study by Julius Petersen.[3] The fourth, extremely brief and superficial, is the introduction to a book by

1. François Mentré, *Les générations sociales* (Paris, 1920).
2. Karl Mannheim, "Das Problem der Generationen," *Kölner Vierteljahrshefte für Soziologie*, 7. Jahrg., Hefte 2–3, 1928.
3. Julius Petersen, *Die literarischen Generationen* (in *Philosophie der Literaturwissenschaft* of Ermatinger [1930]).

Engelbert Drerup.[4] And the last, which reveals superior interpretative methods but is almost completely limited to German and Ortegan contributions to the theme, is the historical portion of a book by Pedro Laín Entralgo, published in 1945.[5] We also find brief, modest historical annotations in works by Pinder and Huizinga, which we shall have occasion to consider later in another connection.

It is not my purpose to write a formal history of the generations theme. I only wish to indicate, as precisely and as concisely as possible, the principal stages in the effort to develop a theory of generations as a concept and principle applicable to historical methodology.[6]

Auguste Comte

So far as I know, Auguste Comte (1798–1857) initiates the scientific study of generations. (Another curious predecessor, to be treated later, cannot be considered a true innovator.) It is not surprising that Comte should be the originator of the generation theory; for, discounting his usual perspicacity and even genius for everything human, the decisive trait in Comte is that he is the first man to have clear ideas about society. And since society is the "setting" or location of generations, as I have pointed out and as we shall see clearly later, it is not until Comte that we have a theoretical basis that will allow the vague and pre-scientific notions of the generation to begin assuming a conceptual existence.

Frequent references to generations appear in Comte's two

4. Engelbert Drerup, *Das Generationsproblem in der griechischen und griechischrömischen Kultur* (Paderborn, 1933).

5. Pedro Laín Entralgo, *Las generaciones en la historia* (Madrid, 1945).

6. At the end of this study I have included some bibliographical references.

principal works. Of course, few of these references have been collected. I shall limit myself to citing the two most important passages, the first from 1839 and the second from 1852.

Comte attempts to determine the causes of the "velocity" of human evolution. After indicating, as does G. Leroy, the element of *ennui,* Comte writes: "I must point out in the second place the *duration of human life* as something which perhaps influences that velocity more than any other appreciable element. In principle we must not lose sight of the fact that *our social progress is essentially dependent on death;* that is, the successive steps of humanity suppose necessarily the continual and sufficiently rapid renewal of the agents of general change. This general change or movement is hardly discernible in the course of an individual life, and only becomes pronounced as *one generation gives way to the following.* In this respect, the social organism is no less subject to the same basic condition as the individual. This means that after a certain amount of time has passed, the different elements of society are transformed by the very nature of life and become unsuited to continue working together as a body. When this happens, the old elements must be replaced by new ones. In any proper consideration of such a social necessity, it would be idle to turn to the illusory supposition of an indefinite duration of human life. Such permanence would quickly lead to the total suppression of progress. Even without going to this extreme, it would be sufficient for such an effect to imagine, for example, that this duration be increased only tenfold. This presupposes, furthermore, that the various natural periods would retain the same respective proportions. If nothing were otherwise changed in the human brain, such a hypothesis would bring about, in my opinion, an inevitable although unmeasurable slowing-down in our social development. For the eternal and indispensable struggle arising spontaneously between the instinct of social conservation, the habitual characteristic of age, and the instinct of innovation, the normal attribute of youth, would then be noticeably altered in favor of the first element in this necessary antagonism. Because of the extreme imperfection of our moral and especially our intellectual nature, those who have contributed most powerfully in their prime to the general progress of the human spirit or society, could not long maintain their rightful predominance without involuntarily becoming more or less hostile to later developments to which they would have ceased to contribute properly. Yet, if on the one hand an overly long duration of human life undoubtedly would tend to retard our social evolution, it is no less certain on the other that a too brief existence would for other reasons prove to be as great an obstacle to general progress. Such a condition would place too much emphasis on the instinct of innovation. For opposing reasons, our social evolution would be therefore equally incompatible with either an excessively slow or an overly rapid renovation of human generations. The extreme shortness of an individual existence, of which scarcely *thirty years* fraught with moral and physical trammels can be fully spent on anything other than *preparations for life or for death,* show clearly in any case the insufficient balance between what a man can reasonably conceive and what he can really achieve" [to this citation and others throughout the book emphasis has been added by means of italicizing—J. M.].[7]

Thirteen years later, in his *System of Positive Politics,* Comte postulates no less than a "positive theory of social alterability." In this context he has to turn anew to the idea of generations: "The modifications of the world can affect humanity directly, even though they are circumscribed within limits that do not perturb life. It is enough that these influences, celestial or terrestrial, continuous or temporary, change to a noticeable degree our

7. Auguste Comte, *Cours de philosophie positive,* 1830–42 Vol. IV, Fifty-first Lesson (Paris, 1839), pp. 635–39.

longevity or the state of human population either in density or movement. Even through the ignorance that still clouds our understanding of the biological laws of longevity, we can see that their influence is not pronounced in the vital order. On the other hand, however, the more modifiable *social order* makes the *ordinary duration of human life* an essential element, not only in its static structure but more especially in its dynamic evolution, in which the rate of change is quite dependent on that duration. Since *the living are essentially governed by the dead,* the *generational interval,* always regulated by common longevity, directly affects the fundamental relationship between subjective and objective influences."[8]

I have quoted these long passages from Comte's works not only because of the interest they have on account of their priority in relation to other books, but also because they are little known and not easily accessible. Comte never says what a generation is. He uses the word not as a technical term but as an ordinary expression of the language understood by all. Yet he has a clear idea of the mechanism through which variations come about in society. In the first place, the decisive factor is death: the limitation imposed on the duration of human life, and with it, the succession of generations. Secondly, that duration of life is quantitatively determined, and the rhythm of evolution depends on it. Thirdly, that duration is articulated in "natural periods" or ages, which exhibit a certain proportion. However, what I have just said is not as important as what I am about to say.

Comte realizes from the outset that this is not properly a question of individual or even family life as such but rather one of *social* phenomena. Thus his point of view transcends genealogy, which, as we shall see, is a preoccupation of most theoreticians on the generations. Comte, in fact, appeals from the outset

8. Ibid., Vol. ii, pp. 447–48.

to two strictly sociological principles, those of conservation and innovation. We must remember that for Comte, private aims and feelings, whatever their social potentialities, are not enough to constitute even "the smallest lasting society" without an intellectual commonwealth arising from "the unanimous adherence to certain fundamental notions."[9] In other words, he sees a system of elemental convictions upon which collective life, maintained or modified by means of successive generational innovations, is based. On the other hand, whereas Comte does not specify the duration of a human generation, the only numerical datum he does give is rigorously exact and the idea unsurpassingly expressed. The period of full exercise of human life—excluding the years spent preparing for life (prior to full social activity) and those lived readying for death (the withdrawal from life)—lasts thirty years. Yet even this limited period is barely attainable, in Comte's view. However, we should not forget that he is writing in 1839, at the end of the Romantic Era, and even that limitation is quite exact. Finally, "the living are governed by the dead." In other words, present human life is conditioned by history; and the articulation of generations, through these precise intervals, regulates government and hence the historical modification of society. Many years will have to pass before we find insights comparable to these first probings by Auguste Comte.

John Stuart Mill

John Stuart Mill (1806–1873), the great English disciple of Auguste Comte, received his idea of generations from him. At a

9. "Whatever the social power one may attribute to common interests, or even to feelings in common, these common interests and feelings would not be sufficient to constitute the smallest durable society, if the intellectual community, brought about by the unanimous agreement on certain fundamental notions, did not intervene at the opportune moment to prevent or correct inevitable customary discord" ibid., p. 679.

very early date, 1843—only four years, that is, after the publication of *Cours de philosophie positive* [Course of Positive Philosophy]—Mill published his famous book on logic: *A System of Logic, Ratiocinative and Inductive.* In considering historical method in this work, Mill devotes several pages to the generations theme and makes specific reference to Comte's ideas. Mill's contribution is of special interest for the date of its appearance certainly, but more particularly because it is perhaps the only English work to deal with the subject—at least I know of no others, either directly or by reference. Nevertheless, by an oddity of fate, it seems to have been forgotten. So far as I can ascertain, only Mentré knows the work, and he scorns it, believing that Mill merely repeats, summarizes, and diminishes what Comte had said.[10] I cannot endorse that judgment, for the few words that Mill devotes to the topic seem to me to be exceedingly precise and penetrating.

"The proximate cause of every state of society," Mill writes, "is the state of society immediately preceding it. The fundamental problem, therefore, of the social science is to find the laws according to which any state of society produces the state which succeeds it and takes its place."[11] Society is understood, then, as a series of successive situations; that is, it is understood historically. "In each successive age," Mill goes on to say, "the principal phenomena of society are different from what they were in the age preceding, and still more different from any previous age: the periods which most distinctly mark these successive changes being *intervals of one generation,* during which a *new set* of human beings have been educated, have grown up from childhood, and *taken possession of society.*"[12] Society is hence stratified

10. Mentré, *Les générations* . . . , p. 75.
11. John Stuart Mill, *A System of Logic, Ratiocinative and Inductive,* Book 6, Chapter 10, par. 2.
12. Ibid., Par. 3 (Marías' italics).

according to the groups that come to the fore in leading it. It is essential to stress the governing character of each new generation that takes possession of society and replaces the preceding generation. Referring to French attempts to discover a law of progress that will allow prediction of the future, Mill points out that it would be a mistake to imagine that this would be a natural law: "It can only be an empirical law. The succession of states of the human mind and of human society cannot have an independent law of its own; it must depend on the psychological and ethnological laws which govern the action of circumstances on men and of men on circumstances."[13] Yet, as Comte noted, it is necessary to link empirical laws derived from history with the laws of human nature.

Mill achieves an even greater precision: "I do not think any one will contend that it would have been possible, setting out from the principles of human nature and from the general circumstances of the position of our species, to determine *a priori* the order in which human development must take place, and to predict, consequently, the general facts of history up to the present time. After the first few terms of the series, *the influence exerted over each generation by the generation which preceded it becomes* (as is well observed by the writer last referred to [Comte]) *more and more preponderant over all other influences;* until at length what we now are and do is in a very small degree the result of the universal circumstances of the human race, or even of our own circumstances acting through the original qualities of our species, but mainly of the qualities produced in us by the *whole previous history of humanity.*"[14] Consequently, "history accordingly does, when judiciously examined, afford Empirical Laws of Society."[15] It is thus necessary to turn

13. Ibid.
14. Ibid., Par. 4. (Marías' italics.)
15. Ibid.

from society to history in order to understand the former; and historical change occurs as a series of influences of preceding generations on those that follow.

There is yet another example of Mill's perspicacity, a very astute methodical indication, the ignorance or neglect of which has allowed the majority of contemporary writers on the generations theme to fall into serious errors. "This branch of the social science," says Mill apropos of the "social dynamic" of Comte, "would be as complete as it can be made if every one of the leading general circumstances of each generation were traced to its causes in the generation immediately preceding. But the *consensus* is so complete (especially in modern history) that, *in the filiation of one generation and another, it is the whole which produces the whole,* rather than any part a part. Little progress, therefore, can be made in establishing the filiation directly from laws of human nature, without having first ascertained the immediate or derivative laws according to which social states generate one another as society advances—the *axiomata media* of General Sociology."[16] Hence a generation is a whole that affects the entire form of society. The abstract derivation of a series of partial "generations"—literary, artistic, political, scientific, etc.—is essentially illusory, and is only of value as an example and as a methodical or didactic simplification. Many weaknesses in the doctrine on generations—as we shall see later—can be traced to these partial sketches.

Mill fails to explain what a generation is, and he does not go into the problem of how long a generation lasts—much less what specific characteristics would serve to identify it. But he does have a perfectly clear idea about the function of generations in the march of history and about their methodological importance.

Within Positivism as a philosophical school *sensu stricto,* and

16. Ibid., Par. 6.

particularly among the sociologists, there are a few echoes of Comte's ideas, but they are of slight interest.

Maximilien Littré (1801–1881) holds that a century is divided into four generations of twenty-five years, and he believes that three of these overlap at any given moment: the old, the adults, and the young. Moreover, he points to four ages in the individual life and establishes a parallel between these and the collective life of humanity. To the four individual ages correspond—rather than the three of Comte's law—four states: the industrial, moral, esthetic, and scientific.[17]

Emile Durkheim (1858–1917), a late representative of positivist sociology, notes the influence of human groupings in social evolution and hence in the generational mechanism. Social change is limited and slow when a generation is strongly subjected to the influence of tradition and the old, and is accelerated when the groupings are larger and men less bound. Change takes place particularly in large cities in which a large part of the population is made up of young mature men who have come there from other places and been separated from their immediate traditions. This explains the mobility and futurism of the great urban centers.[18]

Justin Dromel

With Justin Dromel (born 1826) we enter another world, for he belongs to that second nineteenth-century group concerned with the generations theme. These were not philosophers —discoverers of human life and social reality—but rather men skilled in handling dates, dynasties, and statistics. In 1857 Dromel, a Marseilles lawyer and political writer, published several articles in the *Courrier de Paris* that formed the basis of his book,

17. E. Littré, *Paroles de philosophie positive* (1860).
18. Emile Durkheim, *De la division du travail social* (Paris, 1893).

published in September, 1861, on *La loi des revolutions: les générations, les nationalités, les dynasties, les religions* [The Law of Generations: Generations, Nationalities, Dynasties, Religions], an enormous tome of about six hundred pages that is almost unknown today. Eloquent, declamatory, and pretentious, Dromel is convinced of the importance of his work: "This book," he declares in the first line, "attempts to reveal the future through science."[19] He ends his preface with these words: "For the youth of France, this book will be, I hope, less a call than a prophecy."[20]

Dromel's work is made up of three books and a conclusion: I, "Politics and its Laws"; II, "The Law of Generations"; and III, "Nationalities, Dynasties, and Religions." Book II (pp. 113–314) is the ideological nucleus of the entire work. Its motto is Tacitus' phrase: *Quindecim annos, grande mortalis aevi spatium* (Fifteen years is a long time in human life).[21]

The law of generations is expounded in two chapters, one theoretical, the other historical. The historical chapter purports to be an empirical confirmation of the former, but in reality we find the reverse, as Dromel forges his theory in order to explain a regularity that the study of French political history has revealed to him. Thus are derived the majority of both his insights and his errors. He distinguishes three classes of evolutions: *individual,* ruled by the law of generations; *national,* subject to a dual law (that of nationalities and that of dynasties); and *humanitarian,* ruled in turn by the law of religions. What we have, then, is a general interpretation of the course of humanity, but the decisive element is the social individual—"the individual human mole-

19. Justin Dromel, *La loi des révolutions: les générations, les nationalités, les dynasties, les religions* (Paris, 1861), p. 1.
20. Ibid., p. 7.
21. *De vita Agricolae*, p. 111.

cule endowed with social attraction." The entire system depends, therefore, upon the generations.

Dromel's point of departure is the nation. The highest circle, he says, is Humanity, but Humanity is only a preview, a hope. Nationalities are the present historical reality. Dromel generally confines himself to France, although occasionally he turns to other European nations. Above all else, he is concerned with the duration of individual life in its political and social dimensions rather than in the physical sense. For this purpose, birth may be said to occur at twenty-one, maturity at twenty-five, and a phase of progress from twenty-five to forty. Political life is prolonged to the age of seventy, but activity ceases at about sixty-five. From sixty-five to seventy—and this is an astute observation on Dromel's part—men come under filial influence. Before, the son lived from the father's ideas; now, the father lives from the ideas and ambitions of the son.[22]

Death is the motive force in historical movement. Man is "successional"—subject to death and rebirth. It is for this reason that there is movement in history arising from struggles between one generation and the next. By Dromel's reckoning active life lasts from age twenty-five to sixty-five; thus, if death were to occur all at once to everyone in a generation, the duration of a generation would be forty years, and each generation would be replaced in a single stroke by the one following. Since death occurs gradually, however, things happen differently. For a generation to decline, it need not have disappeared. It is enough that it be in the minority, and this would be the case if the death rate were maintained regularly at mid-point (at the twenty-year mark). This consideration reduces the length of the political generation to this last figure, but it must needs be reduced still further.

22. Ibid., pp. 117–23.

At this point statistics intervene. Dromel divides the French population of 1851 and 1856 into five periods: the first, up to the age of twenty-one, is politically inactive; the second, from twenty-one to twenty-five, represents the phase of political apprenticeship; the third and fourth, which comprise the years from twenty-five to sixty-five, are those of active life; and the fifth, made up of those over sixty-five, corresponds to the phase of waning interest, old-age, and political death, and in terms of numbers is naturally comparatively small. The decisive portion is made up of the third and fourth periods. This portion is really two because within the active period Dromel distinguishes two phases, ascendent and declining, each of which is at odds with the other. In any age there are, therefore, two fully active human groups engaged in a great political debate. On the one hand, there are those who struggle to gain power, and on the other hand, those who have power but are gradually losing it. Such is Dromel's most penetrating idea, but his socio-political suppositions cloud his thinking. For in fact Dromel believes that the decisive factor is the rule of majorities and minorities. Hence it is statistics that separate the years belonging to the two periods. There are approximately as many men from twenty-five to forty-one as there are from forty-two to sixty-five. This, then, is the dividing line. Ascendent political life lasts sixteen years; the declining years number twenty-four. This difference is determined by the date when the young ascendent generation becomes a majority.[23]

23. "From the ages of twenty-five to sixty-five occur ascendent and descendent political life. The combination of the two phases will form what we shall call the great active period in politics. . . . It is within this period, and among the men who constitute it, that the great political debate will be staged, even though the majority decision will serve as the dénouement, that is, the power of those who rule in our modern societies (the majority being half

This number sixteen is the duration of generations. However, it is not an immutable figure. The average duration of physical —hence political—life tends to increase. Before the nineteenth century, the duration of a generation was probably fifteen years. A half century later, Dromel says, it is at least sixteen.[24]

The law of generations, thus understood, establishes the mechanism of change in majorities. For Dromel the "majority" is synonymous with public opinion. Therefore, any opinion, any system or institution lasts as long as the majority under which it was established lasts (about sixteen years).[25] Different ages really correspond to different opinions.[26] Hence the individual and his entire generation have a certain inflexibility, in the sense that they remain faithful to their own principles.[27]

Dromel summarizes his law of generations in four concrete principles:

1. The predominance of a generation lasts some sixteen years, after which a new generation succeeds it in power.

---

plus one). This great period of activity must be divided into two equal parts, according to the number of individuals included in it, in order to give birth to the third and fourth periods, which we shall call in the first case the period of *ascendent political life,* in the other, *descendent political life.* The dividing point is age forty-one. Hence the first period lasts some sixteen years, and the other about twenty-four" (*La loi* . . . , pp. 145–46).

24. Ibid., p. 148.

25. "Any opinion, any system, any political establishment will last as long as the majority that presided over its making, with a period of sixteen years the normal maximum" (Ibid., p. 154).

26. "We must establish that different ages correspond truly and inexorably to different opinions and to a different political ideal. In other words, we have had reason to group individuals according to their ages, since the group made up of all the individuals of the same age will certainly correspond to a particular political opinion . . ." (Ibid., p. 155).

27. Ibid., pp. 178–79.

2. During a generation's dominance, the one to follow completes its political education and criticizes its predecessor.

3. A generation's social ideal is superior to, and in a sense in conflict with, that of its predecessor.

4. The work of each generation is special, unique, uniform, and exclusive.[28]

Such is the theoretical substance of his law, which Dromel tries to justify historically. In French history of the preceding eighty years, he classifies the following political periods: 1789–1800, 1800–1815, 1815–1830, and 1830–1848, each period lasting almost exactly fifteen years. Of the first period he notes that strictly speaking it should date from at least as early as 1787. As for the last, he believes the resistance of those in power caused a delay in the normal evolution. If this law is not observed so clearly and precisely in European countries other than France, Dromel maintains, it is because they lack on the one hand, method and rational capacity, and on the other, the juridical and practical development enjoyed by the individual in France after 1789. But Dromel is confident that other nations will eventually (and with increasing exactness) observe this fifteen- or sixteen-year generational law.[29]

28. Ibid., p. 185.
29. It is curious to note what Dromel thinks of generations in Spain. Above all, they are completely independent of those in the rest of Europe, because Spain is isolated from Europe not only by geography but even more by ideas. Besides, there is a great irregularity, apparently, in their political evolution. Spain will be the last Latin nation to adjust to the cadence of normal progress. Dromel indicates a series of dates in Spanish politics of the nineteenth century, principally 1808, 1812, 1820, 1823, 1834, 1845, 1860, which appear to belie the law of fifteen or sixteen sequences. Dromel's explanation is this: all Spanish movements are incomplete and abortive, and owing to unfulfillment of the law of generations, Spain is in a state of quasi-revolutionary effervescence, of

Dromel offers two marginal observations that are of some interest here. The singlemindedness and exclusiveness that are characteristic of a generation's accomplishments tend to be surpassed by that very generation itself. Thus, a capacity for evolving may be expected of the human generation itself, resulting in its historical efficiency being prolonged and its resistence to the innovations of the following generation being reduced. Furthermore, generations are succeeded and associated with each other in pairs, thus forming groups who live under the same ideal and set the framework for "a more general fusion in the unity of progress."[30]

Dromel is far from making a *theory* of generations—we shall see that only once has it been possible to do this—and his *exposé théorique* is quite untheoretical and incapable of withstanding analysis. However, aside from his overweening insistence on the theme, his insights are not unimportant. For one thing, he is the first to shun genealogy and to devote himself resolutely to the concept of collective life. True, he restricts his thought to political life, concerned as he was with anticipating French political crises. This is where his interest lay, and it tends to make his idea seem somewhat more trivial than it otherwise might. Nevertheless, he presents the problem in terms that go beyond the notion of the physical generation and the thirty-year distance between parents and children. In the second place, he offers a workable, and not merely biological, diagram of the different human ages: he sees them as different "rôles" played in political life. In the

---

pronunciamientos and conspiracies. Its energy is thus spent, so that when a new generation appears, its leaders, or those who would be leaders, are already ineffective. The triumph of the *vicalvaristas* [a liberal faction] in 1854, says Dromel, has destroyed in advance the future revolution of Spain; instead of a deep and radical movement, there will be partial, almost meaningless agitations. See ibid., pp. 298–301.

30. Ibid., pp. 533–34.

third place, his idea of the ascending and declining phases in the period of greatest activity, and the attendant problem of dynamic balance, is extremely acute. Finally, emphasis should be placed on the fifteen- or sixteen-year figure given as the duration of a generation. But here it should be noted that Dromel has followed a plan that is the reverse of his exposition. Having discovered the fifteen-year periods empirically, he constructs his theory to explain them. This is evident in the fact that when his theory places the number at twenty, he has to employ an ingenious expedient —the mortality rate and the changes in majorities—in order to lower it to sixteen and thus approach the empirical data that engendered the theory. It is in this that the weakness in Dromel's thought is found, because the loss of power is not solely a consequence of the shifting of majorities. His singleminded attention to politics, and especially democratic politics dependent on the ballot, permits him to be satisfied with this explanation. This limits the regularity of the law of generations to those countries and times with this kind of politics and thus effectively denies its appealing simplicity. Dromel does not and indeed cannot know the place of generations, even though he has a vague notion arising from his close contact with historical material. Hence he cannot explain the very truths he has glimpsed, and his concepts are ultimately superficial and insufficient. Thus, although he declines to present the problem in individual biographical terms—and thus avoids an error into which some later thinkers will fall—but rather associates the problem with collective life, on the other hand, he abides by visible political changes instead of attempting to explain generations in terms of the total structure of society.

A Precedent: Soulavie

The idea of the fifteen-year period, and its application to French political history, has a precedent much earlier than Dromel's formulation and which predates any scientific treatment of the problem of generations. Jean-Louis Giraud, a French naturalist and historian known as Soulavie (1753–1813), who studied both fossil distribution in geological strata and periodicity in eighteenth century French history, was apparently the first to interpret generations as human groupings that succeed each other in power and control every fifteen years.[31] Soulavie distinguishes six generations in the eighteenth century, men "whose character and principles have attracted the attention of all enlightened peoples because of the great events they have prepared." Each of these generations lasts fifteen years, after which it seemingly exhausts itself and surrenders its place to the following group. The periods pointed out by Soulavie are: 1700–1715 (the old age of Louis XIV); 1715–1726 (the regency of Phillip of Orleans and the ministry of the Duke of Bourbon); 1726–1742 (Cardinal Fleury); 1742–1756 (Madame de Pompadour

31. J. L. Soulavie, *Pièces inédites sur les règnes de Louis XIV, Louis XV et Louis XVI* (Paris, 1809). This is the work cited by Benloew and—apparently indirectly though the latter's work—by Mentré. But antecedents are to be found in another curious work of Soulavie, an older work entitled: *Tableaux de l'histoire de la décadence de la monarchie française, et des progrès de l'autorité royale à Copenhague, Madrid, Vienne, Stockolm, Berlin, Pétersbourg, Londres, depuis l'époque où Louis XIV fut surnommé le Grand jusqu'à la mort de Louis XVI* (Paris, 1803). The main part of this book is composed of several great synoptic panoramas, the second of which shows the stages referred to as generations in the later writing. The third picture or panorama deals with the thirty-five families making up the Republic of Letters in France from Francis I to 1800. It is a detailed chronology with hundreds of names and including all disciplines. The dates given are those of the person's death, although this is not always indicated. This book reveals meticulous care, almost an obsession with detail and with long lists of dates and names. Accordingly, he shows a great familiarity with the data that could serve as the basis for a systemizing of history by generations.

and Count Steinbach); 1756–1774 (the Duke of Choiseul); 1774–1789 (Louis XVI); and 1789–1800 (Revolution).

Dromel was not aware of Soulavie—or at least he does not cite him. Louis Benloew, on the other hand, made frequent reference to Soulavie's work. Benloew, a French Jewish professor, was dean of the Faculty of Letters at Dijon and published a book on the laws of history.[32] Benloew believes history to be divided into long cycles of fifteen hundred years, each of which is divided into three hundred-year periods with subdivisions of a hundred and fifty years. His computations and the ample generalizations that accompany them are totally inconsistent. The only items of interest in his work, which is of slight value, in general, are his scheme of human ages and the seventh chapter of Book Five ("The Calendar of History"), which is devoted to "fifteen-year evolutions."

Benloew considers a life fulfilled when it reaches the age of seventy-five. He divides this figure into five ages of fifteen years each. During the first, one's faculties are still commingled with the body; during the second, imagination predominates; during the third, will; during the fourth, reason; and finally, during the fifth, the plenitude of reason.[33]

In France since the Revolution, says Benloew, the form of government changes every fifteen or sixteen years. A political generation, then, would last only half as long as the time Homer attributed to the human generation.[34] This establishes the elemental structure of history in terms of fifteen-year evolutions, representing the virile and vigorous activity of a generation.[35] Benloew refers constantly to Soulavie, but he attempts to extend

32. Louis Benloew, *Les lois de l'histoire* (Paris, 1881).
33. Ibid., pp. 264–65.
34. Ibid., p. 267. Benloew accepts the commonplace and indeed trivial idea that in France, after the Revolution, the government changes every fifteen years.
35. Ibid., pp. 291–92.

his calculations to history before France, to England, Greece, and Rome. The result is the following.

France, 1515–1700: twelve evolutions in a hundred and eighty-five years, with a mean of fifteen years and five months.

England, 1625–1760: nine evolutions in a hundred and thirty-five years, with a mean of fifteen years.

Greece, 510–301 B.C.: thirteen evolutions; and Rome, 300–31 B.C.: nineteen evolutions, for a grand total of thirty-two evolutions in four hundred and eighty years, with a mean of fifteen years.[36]

Such are Benloew's ideas. Clearly he did not know what a generation is or why it lasts fifteen years. But his work does offer proof of a historical regularity on a larger scale than that provided by Soulavie, though the latter was his source of inspiration and the only precedent he knew.

Antoine Cournot

In 1868 Cournot (1801–1877) wrote his *Considérations sur la marche des idées et des événements dans les temps modernes* [Considerations on the Course of Ideas and Events in Modern Times]. In the eighth chapter of Book One of this work, which was published in 1872, the author poses the problem of historical divisions and attempts to eliminate the arbitrary element in an effort to discover "natural" divisions that are not merely conventional but correspond to "real changes in the flow of ideas and the course of events." Cournot tries to discover some meaning in the century as a historical unit: "If, according to the opinion of the most ancient writers and in accord with modern observations, it is thought that a century presents approximately three active generations coming one after another, one begins to glimpse the possibility of a natural relation." As for the duration

36. Ibid., pp. 294–300.

of a generation, then, Cournot accepts the traditional idea
handed down from the Greeks. But he adds some refinements of
his own concerning the instrument of change from one generation to the next: "Each generation transmits to the one immediately following a certain wealth of ideas through education; and
while this educative process or transmission is taking place, the
educating generation is still present and is still influenced by all
the survivors of a previous generation which continues to play an
important part in the government of the society and in the flow
of ideas and business. Nor have the survivors of earlier generations lost all domestic authority (notwithstanding what taciturn
censors may have said in all ages, especially our own). The youth
being initiated into the world also bear, more than their pre-
sumptuousness would allow them to believe, the imprint of childhood impressions made during conversations with the elderly."[37]
Hence there are always three generations present and interacting,
and since for Cournot the three totaled equal a century, the latter
has real historical significance. But this is not as simple as it
seems. "In society, certainly, *all ages are mixed,* all transitions are
continuous; *generations are not placed one after another,* as in a
genealogical chart. Therefore, *only the observation of historical
facts* can accurately show us how *the gradual renovation of ideas
results from the imperceptible replacement of older generations
by the younger,* and how much time is necessary for the change
to become noticeable enough to distinguish clearly one period
from another."[38]

37. A. Cournot, *Considérations sur la marche des idées et des
événements dans les temps modernes* (Paris, 1872), Book 1,
Chapter VIII.
38. Ibid. Cournot appears to allude to Dromel's work when he
says: "In our time some try to explain the hints of periodicity believed found in the rapid succession of certain political crises by
the law or mortality."

Cournot goes on to consider the point-of-departure problem: if he can establish a starting point, he will then be able to determine the actual succession of real generations. His guiding notion is the century, however, and he is bound by its limits. Moreover, the only methodical indication given by him is the one cited earlier, which is accurate as far as it goes but excessively vague: the necessity of being guided by the observation of historical facts.

With Cournot the French contribution to the generation theme essentially ends. An exception must be made of Mentré, who, as a distant disciple of Cournot, expanded the latter's ideas. Otherwise, the French contribution, though certainly of value, has been largely forgotten.

Giuseppe Ferrari

A new doctrine of generations, contemporaneous with those just discussed, is that of Giuseppe Ferrari (1812–1876), an Italian closely connected with French positivistic thought and influenced, as was Dromel, by Auguste Comte, and who was also a student of Vico and a disciple of Giovanni Romagnosi. As a man of advanced political ideas, and specifically as an advocate of a federal republic in Italy, Ferrari was obliged to live elsewhere. He took up residence in Paris and it was there that he published most of his books. Interested in the school of Saint-Simon, influenced by Pierre Leroux, and progressive in the manner of the times, Ferrari concentrated all his attention on political history. The vast amount of bibliographical and other informative material he handled was great, notwithstanding the conceptual limitations of his thought. His central idea is that of political periods, and his attempts to identify such periods soon led him to the study of generations.

Ferrari's theory "sulla misure del tempo e sul meccanismo delle rivoluzioni" [of the measure of time and the mechanism of revolutions] is born, in his own words, in his *Histoire des révolutions d'Italie* [History of Revolutions in Italy] (Paris, 1856–58); developed in *Histoire de la raison d'État* [History of the Reason of the State] (Paris, 1860), expanded in *La Chine et l'Europe, leur histoire et leurs traditions comparées* [China and Europe, A Comparison of their History and Traditions] (Paris, 1867); and reaches its plenitude in his most important book, *Teoria dei periodi politici* [Theory of Political Periods] (Milan, 1874). Preliminary and partial developments of the theory may be found in his *Philosophie de la révolution* [Philosophy of Revolution] (1851), as well as in *Corso sugli scrittori politici italiani* [Course on Italian Political Writers] (1862), in articles published in his *Nuova Antologia* [New Anthology] (1870–71), and in a course on Byzantine history taught at the University of Rome and published in *Il Diritto* [On Law] (1876). I shall deal here with the clear antecedents of this theory found in *Histoire de la raison d'État* and its mature development in *Teoria dei periodi politici.*

In the first of these books, Ferrari devotes a chapter to "the periods of history" in which he asseverates the constant rule that every thirty years the historical scene changes, and that each generation strives blindly to overthrow the government and to rule in turn.[39] Now although each thirty-year phase is a complete drama of itself, it is at the same time only *one act* of a much vaster play. Revolution occurs in two stages: first, destruction of traditional government, second, reconstruction with new men and ideas. Since each revolution is followed by a period of reaction, with its negative and constructive stages, every histori-

39. "By an unchanging law, every thirty years the scene changes, each generation works blindly in a political effort aimed at overwhelming or overturning the government, and to supplant that government with ideas hitherto unknown by it" Giuseppe Ferrari, *Histoire de la raison d'État* (Paris, 1860), p. 211.

cal period comprises four intervals: 1. a subversive period, 2. a solution, 3. a struggle against that solution, and 4. a final victory that confirms it.[40] Ferrari concludes that since the year 1000, four intervals of thirty years each have formed periods that run their course in a hundred and twenty or twenty-five years.[41] Every five hundred years an extraordinary movement occurs, revealing that the one-hundred-twenty-five-year periods are but acts of a still larger drama.[42]

These nascent ideas, only rudimentarily outlined in the *Histoire* . . . , are developed in greater deail in *Teoria dei periodi politici*. In the first and most interesting part of the book, "La generazione pensante" [the thinking generation] is treated. In the second part, he deals with "Il periodo in quattro tempi" [the

40. "However, if each phase of thirty years each contains a complete drama, it is still only a stirring, a step in the march of nations, an act within a longer play. We have seen that all revolution occurs in two parts: the first destroys the traditional government; the other rebuilds it with new men and new ideas. These are two distinct phases. The man who lives during the first phase is not at all prepared for the second phase when he will be sacrificed. We have also seen that each revolution is inevitably followed by a period of reaction, which is in turn subdivided into a time of negative government and a striving toward a resolution according to a formula that offers protection against foreign powers. This leads to two other phases, so that each period is composed of the four intervals of subversion, solution, divisive combat, and reassuring victory" (ibid., pp. 213–14).

41. "To sum up, it is enough to say that from 1800 on, four intervals of thirty years each always make up a period that runs its course in a hundred twenty or a hundred twenty-five years" (ibid., p. 216).

42. "Every hundred five years an extraordinary movement announces that each period of a hundred twenty-five years is, in turn, but an act of a still longer play more in keeping with the life of nations" (ibid., p. 217).

period (divided) into four times], in the third, "Le contradizioni politiche" [political contradictions], and in the fourth, "La velocità comparata" [comparative rate (of change)], all followed by a hundred pages of statistical, chronological, and biographical appendices.

Ferrari's starting point is the "generation," which is the primary element in the process of historical recurrence, and which repeats the same drama in every age. It is, then, the elemental movement of history.[43] Rather than being a generation in the physical sense, which would imply merely a coincidence in time, the political generation is composed of *men who are born, who live and die in the same years, and who, whether friends or enemies, belong to the same society.* This political or historical generation presupposes, unlike the physical or biological generation, a collaboration in the same undertakings.[44]

In determining the duration of generations it is not enough to consider only the average human life span. The latter turns out to be, according to Ferrari's data, about thirty years. But this figure is attributable to the fact that at least half of the people in any generation die in their early years before they are old enough to be of historical consequence. A generation is not wholly replaced at the age of thirty, since older men are always in power. This means that a generation must be considered as a political reality, which is to say that it begins at the moment

43. "For us the generation is the prime element of ebb and flow. Like the rising and setting of the sun, it always remains the same; it continually repeats the same drama in all times and in all civilizations. It is born, lives, and dies . . . The generation will serve as our point of departure" Giuseppe Ferrari, *Teoria dei periodi politici* (Milan, 1874), pp. 7–8.

44. "Its basic political condition is that it consists of men who are born, who live and die, in the same years, and who, friends or enemies of each other, belong to the same society" (ibid., p. 8).

when men arrive at, or are born into, political life. We may ascertain this moment through the biographies of superior men who are "i capi della società, i re del pensiero, i signori della generazione" [the heads of society, the kings of thought, and the lords of the generation]. The average duration of public life, which begins from the twentieth to the twenty-fifth year for artists and at about the age of thirty for philosophers, jurists, and historians, is some thirty years and a few months. Outstanding men, therefore, have a life twice as long as the average: to the thirty years considered as an average life span must be added the thirty belonging to history.[45]

Every thirty years, then, generations and their governments are renewed, new actions begin, a new drama unfolds with new characters. It is the advent of a new period.[46] Men of an exceptionally long life, says Ferrari, really live two lives. They belong to two generations; they change style, direction, and inspiration. The examples of Voltaire, Goethe, Aristophanes, and Sophocles confirm this.[47] If a man lived two thousand years like the Count of Cagliostro, from Cana's wedding to the orgies of Louis XV, he would still have to begin life anew every thirty years.[48]

But what are the definitive criteria of a generation, and what determines whether a man belongs to a particular one? At this point Ferrari makes unrestrained use of his great presupposition: politics rules the world. All that really counts is the political change that accompanies the generations. Consequently, changes in governments establish the real scale, and because of this one must start in a country with actual political dates. The birth of Jesus Christ cannot be taken as a date in Roman history; it was merely something that happened during the fourteenth year of

45. Ibid., pp. 9–15.
46. Ibid., p. 16.
47. Ibid., p. 74 ff.
48. Ibid., p. 80.

Tiberius' rule. Rather one must calculate the generational series *ab urbe condita,* not only for Rome but also for others—Egypt, Persia, or China, for example. Within a particular culture, political men and their governments determine both the name and the limits of each generation. Lesser men, says Ferrari, are situated in the generation where they have spent most of their public life. Unhindered by potential pitfalls in his theory, Ferrari offers in the next breath nothing less as examples than Descartes and Malebranche. Descartes spent twenty-eight of his thirty-two years of public life in Richelieu's generation; hence, he necessarily belongs to it. Malebranche spent thirty out of forty-one years in the reactionary period of Louis XIV.[49] Neither Socrates nor Jesus Christ is a decisive figure in this sense because they were not politicians and did not bring about changes in governments.

These generations, lasting an average of some thirty-one years and three months—no more and no less—are not homogeneous; rather, they assume different historical roles in a larger drama that lasts a hundred and twenty-five years.[50] Each principle needs four generations or acts during which it completes its total evolution and brings its cycle to a close.[51] The first generation of a period is preliminary or preparatory, the second is revolutionary or explosive, the third is reactionary, and the fourth is harmonizing.[52] While generations may vary between twenty and

49. "Inferior men identify themselves with the generation in which they spent the greatest number of years of their political life. Of his thirty-two years of public life, Descartes spent twenty-eight in Richelieu's generation, and he belongs to it necessarily. And since Malebranche spent thirty of his forty-one years of public life in the Reaction of Louis XIV, there is where he must be placed" (ibid., p. 66).
50. Ibid., p. 102.
51. Ibid., p. 113.
52. Ibid., p. 182.

forty-five years, the longer periods are quite regular, varying at
the extreme from a hundred to a hundred and fifty years, with
the majority falling between a hundred and eleven and a
hundred and thirty-six years.[53]

Such, in its most condensed form, is Ferrari's theory. Extrava-
gant as it undoubtedly is, it merits more than simple oblivion or
a scornful mention by Croce.[54] Ferrari surpasses in fact, though
not in principle or with full self-awareness of his achievement,
the genealogical point of view, and he defines generations precisely in terms of a historical function. Unfortunately, he limits
this function to politics and thereby forecloses any understanding
or explanation of historical reality in its deepest meanings. Moreover, despite the apparent objectivity with which the cycles are
studied, the duration of generations is determined through individual life, by a normal extension of each man's active life.
Hence, Ferrari disregards what is most decisive, which is—as we
shall see in time—the interaction of contemporaneous generations. Finally, the great discovery of Ferrari, which is to attribute
a task, a destiny or mission, to each generation—that is, to give
each of them a *historical* reality—is very nearly invalidated by
the formalistic and inertial tendency of his thought. Because all
historical variation is made to follow a preconceived notion of a
four-phase cycle that is endlessly repeated, this same variation is
ipso facto distorted and voided. Strictly speaking, all the deficiencies in Ferrari's theory spring from his vague grasp of what a
generation is: men who are born at a certain time, who live and
die *in the same years.* But just which years are these, and what are
their boundaries? To this most decisive question Ferrari offers no
answer. The vagueness of his idea is necessarily increased by the

53. Ibid., p. 254.
54. Cf. Benedetto Croce, *Teoria e storia della storiografia,* 2nd.
ed. (Bari, 1920), p. 101.

lack of a precise determination of a generation's beginning. And since he cannot determine intrinsically the nature of a generation, he is forced to turn to its most visible and apparent features, namely political changes. But the very visibility and manifest quality of politics indicate that it is only a superficial reflection of true historical reality.

Gustav Rümelin

As we have seen, the scientific study of generations was begun rather early in France. We have also found an early—and, so far as I know, the only—English contribution which, despite Mill's usual keen perception, cannot conceal its immediate source in Comte. And Ferrari, although Italian by birth, was immersed in the culture of France, where he lived after 1838. Therefore, contrary to what some recent German writers and those influenced by them have maintained, the theory of generations is "German" neither in origin nor in development. As we shall see later, neither can the only fully developed theory of generations to date be considered German.

The early German attempts to deal with the generations theme were made almost simultaneously and originated in three different fields: statistics, philosophy, and history. The first effort, which has much in common with the work of Dromel and Ferrari, was that of Gustav Rümelin (1815–1889), the author of an essay entitled *Über den Begriff und die Dauer einer Generation* [On the Concept and Duration of a Generation].[55]

Rümelin, who was a professor, a publicist, and a politician, was born in Ravensburg (Württemberg) and studied in the

55. This essay was published in Volume 1 of Rümelin's *Reden und Aufsätze* (Tübingen, 1875), pp. 285–304. Volumes 2 and 3 were published in Freiburg im Breisgau in 1881. A French translation of the work exists entitled: *Problèmes d'économie politique et de statistique* (Paris, 1896), pp. 153–71.

48

Protestant seminary of Schönthal and at the University of Tübingen (1832–36), where he was a disciple of Ferdinand Baur, David Strauss, and Friedrich Vischer. He devoted himself to classical philology and later, drawn to social studies, published essays and pamphlets and held important public posts. After 1867 he was professor of statistics and psychology at Tübingen while simultaneously directing the statistical services of Württemberg. He was a man active in statistical work and familiar with his materials, but with a theoretical inclination and training.

Rümelin discovers two meanings in the word "generation": 1) men presently alive, and 2) the distance between those ascending and those declining as a measure of time. The second meaning is that of genealogy. Statistically stated, the duration of a generation is "the mean of the age differences between *parents* and children during a given period." Rümelin further states that he is referring to fathers only, rather than to a mean including both fathers and mothers. On the other hand, he makes no distinction between sons and daughters. Were he to include mothers, he would have to alter his calculations. Moreover, all his ideas are restricted to monogamous societies among civilized peoples. In those countries of early puberty, polygamy, and slavery the offspring of the same father can be up to fifty years apart in age. In these societies, it would not be possible to trace generations, at least not in the way Rümelin understands them.

In precise statistical terms, the duration of a generation may be calculated as follows: the average age of the husband at marriage plus half of the average number of fertile years of the marriage. In fact, a year must be added to the father's age at marriage (this is the time that normally passes before the birth of the first child) and subtracted from the fertile period.

This duration varies from country to country. Rümelin obtains the following results:

Germany . . . . 30 + 1 + 11/2 = 36½
England . . . . 28 + 1 + 13/2 = 35½
France . . . . 30 + 1 + 7/2 = 34½
United States, Russia, Australia . . 25 + 1 + 13/2 = 32½
Less advanced countries . . . . . 34 + 1 + 8/2 = 39

Young, developing peoples have short generations; older, more complex countries with limited resources are characterized by longer generations. This difference reveals important consequences. If we have, for example, a lifetime of seventy years, and if the age difference between fathers and children is thirty-five or thirty-six years, then only two generations can coexist at any given time. But if this difference is lowered to twenty-eight or thirty years, there is time for two and a half generations. In other words, the young have access to their grandparents until adolescence and thus can see the vanishing generation with their own eyes.

Besides this statistical and demographic interest, Rümelin shows an awareness of the historical import of the concept of generations: "A century is an imposing and obscure temporal magnitude which surpasses our native grasp. The generation, on the other hand, is an intuitive and comprehensible span of time to us. The sum total of universal history is brought humanly nearer and made more coherent if we imagine it in terms of how many times we must retravel the familiar road leading from the son to the father. The difference between the opinions and ideas of parents and children seems relatively small to us. It is rather like a nuance within the same fundamental color. It may surprise us, then, to realize that we only have to triple that difference and reduce it to a specific figure in order to go back all the way to Frederick the Great, Voltaire, Klopstock, and Lessing; and if we multiply it by seven we find ourselves transported back to a

completely different system of European states and to the min
of Gustavus Adolphus, Cromwell, Richelieu, and the Grai
Elector. Thirty generations ago our ancestors might still be saci
ficing horses to Thor and Odin; sixty generations ago they wou
be leading their flocks through the pasturelands of central Asi
It is not violent revolutions and volcanic eruptions that tran
form human life in periodic thrusts; rather the small differenc
between parents and children in customs and ways of looking ;
things are generalized to a point of mass effect. We call th
content and progression of such effects the cultural history (
mankind."[56]

Rümelin does not look beyond the genealogical idea of th
generation except when individual cases force him to turn t
large statistical numbers. Only in this secondary and nonessentia
sense could it be said that he moves in the area of collective life
in other words, we can surmise that his statistics is a statistics o
genealogical generations, referring in the final analysis to indi
viduals, even though a great many individuals are considered
The latter point is decisive. The most valuable parts of Rümelin':
doctrine are, first, his clear awareness that historical change is
above all, the normal variation occurring in a series of generations, and second, his postulate of a historical method of investigation based on the study of these elemental changes and thei
concatenation throughout time.

Wilhelm Dilthey

A new point of view on the problem of generations is inau-
gurated with Wilhelm Dilthey (1833–1911). Comte began his
study of the concept of generations from the perspective of social
reality; Dilthey happens upon the concept while exploring his
great discovery: human life. These two contributions are the most

56. *Reden und Aufsätze,* pp. 303–304.

profound of the nineteenth century, and in a certain sense both of them have suffered the same fate, that of being noticed little and late. Comte's work has yet to be adequately investigated and interpreted even now, despite the enormous spread of positivism in the nineteenth century, and his ideas on the generations, apart from their immediate repercussion in John Stuart Mill, have rarely even been cited. As for Dilthey, it is all too well known that he was "discovered" just a few years ago. If one looks at a bibliography of works on Dilthey, one sees that except for a few studies published in 1911 or thereabouts, around the time of his death, virtually nothing appeared until early in the 1930's. The circumstantial reason for this "revival" was his centennial in 1933, but the deeper explanation is that not until that time did philosophy reach a level that made it possible for the scope of Dilthey's work to be understood.

The idea of the generations appears in Dilthey at a relatively early period. He outlined the concept, but without ever developing it, in works written between the ages of thirty-two and forty-two. Yet in one of his last writings, dating from a year before his death, he refers to his old idea and enumerates the times he has studied it.[57] The first text, dated 1865, is an essay on Novalis.[58] He takes up the notion again in 1867, in his beginning lesson at Basel, *Die dichterische und philosophische Bewegung in Deutschland 1770–1800* [The Poetic and Philosophical Movement in Germany from 1770 to 1800];[59] again in 1867–1870 in

---

57. Wilhelm Dilthey, *Der Aufbau der geschichtlichen Welt in den Geisteswissenschaften* (1910), in Vol. 7 of *Gesammelte Schriften*.

58. It was first published in the *Preussische Jahrbücher,* and later included in the tome *Das Erlebnis und die Dichtung* (1905). My references are to the Spanish translation in *Vida y poesía* (Mexico, 1945), pp. 339–402.

59. Published in *Gesammelte Schriften,* Vol. 5.

52

Das Leben Schleiermachers [Schleiermacher's Life];[60] and finally
—and more profoundly—in 1875, in *Über das Studium der
Geschichte der Wissenschaften vom Menschen, der Gesellschaft
und dem Staat* [On the Study of the History of the Sciences of
Man, Society, and the State].[61]

Dilthey undertakes the study of Novalis with "the great hope
of being able to clarify in him some of the more important
motives in the conception of the world appearing in the *generation* that follows Goethe, Kant, and Fichte."[62] He goes on to say:
"The conditions that influence the intellectual culture of a generation are truly countless and limitless. Let us group these conditions around two factors. In the first place, there appears in a
certain way *the patrimony of intellectual culture which this
generation encounters at the time that it seriously begins to shape
itself.* When the generation being shaped assumes control of, and
attempts to surmount, the spiritual accumulation of its patrimony, it finds itself already under the influence of the second of
the factors being considered: that of the *surrounding life,* the
factor of the relationships that form society and make up political and social states, all of which are infinitely diverse. This
implies certain limits on the possibilities of further progress
offered by every preceding generation."[63]

"Now then," continues Dilthey, "what method is suggested
here for the study of the intellectual culture of a period? We can
only suggest it at this point. *An extraordinarily promising concept for this purpose, which certainly would have to be treated in*

60. Only the first volume of the *Life of Schleiermacher* was
published.
61. It was published in *Philosophische Monatshefte* and included in *Gesammelte Schriften,* Vol. 5.
62. "Novalis" in *Vida y poesía,* p. 342.
63. Ibid., p. 342.

greater depth, is the generation. The most fortunate case would be when one of these generations appears so clearly delineated that it may be said that it is a matter of making a study of it. Such is the case we find before us now. A. G. Schlegel, Schleiermacher, Alexander von Humboldt, Hegel, Novalis, Friedrich Schlegel, Hölderlin, Wackenroder, Tieck, Fries, and Schelling all reveal most markedly, in the first decade of their appearance on the scene, the influence of the conditions under which they were jointly raised."[64]

The names cited by Dilthey are chronologically grouped in a brief period of time that does not span a decade. A. G. Schlegel was born in 1767; Schleiermacher 1768; Humboldt in 1769; Hegel and Hölderin in 1770; Novalis and the younger of the Schlegels in 1772; Wackenroder, Tieck, and Fries in 1773; Schelling—and his extraordinary precociousness must be taken into account—in 1775. This concentration of dates turns out to be quite favorable for Dilthey, for as we shall see, he is not very sure about the limits of a generation or about the method of determining them.

Dilthey goes on to observe: "Nevertheless, among these men *extraordinary differences* exist regarding the elements of intellectual culture. . . . Keeping in mind this *complete heterogeneity,* the problem of knowing how, under these conditions, *a closed circle of men, a defensive and offensive alliance, a school,* could be formed, would turn out to be extraordinarily interesting."[65] And showing "how loose was the woof in which the first threads were interwoven," Dilthey adds: "Not only because of the force with which the divergencies of existing tendencies were felt, but also because there were no cordial relationships on a personal

64. Ibid., p. 343.
65. Ibid., pp. 358–59.

basis. What held them together was the advantages derived from a defensive–offensive alliance against the outworn albeit immortal tendencies of the Nicolais, the Hubers, and the Schützes."[66]

In his course at Basel, Dilthey makes use of the concept of the generation without trying to explain it, in order to understand a period of German spiritual history. He distinguishes three generations. The first is represented by Lessing (born in 1729), and the second by Goethe (born in 1749) and Schiller (1759). The third is divided into two groups, that of Berlin, represented by Schleiermacher (1768), Gentz (1764), Tieck (1773), and Bernhardi (1769); and that centered around Schelling (1775) and Hegel (1770). These dates must be kept in mind. Dilthey uses a metaphor of waves to explain the arrival of new generations: "eine neue Welle trug die beiden Männer empor . . ." [a new wave carried both men up]. The idea of the *connection* of generations, which Dilthey adds to the mere characterization of one, such as in the case of Novalis, is essential.[67]

In 1875 Dilthey formulated a more precise and complete concept of the generation. The course of spiritual movements, seen from without, can be ordered in a chronological system of hours, months, years, and decades. But the unity through which we intuitively apprehend that course must be rooted in ourselves. An inner measure of psychic time corresponds to the seconds and minutes of a clock; "human life" and the progression of its "ages" correspond to the decades and centuries of historical movement. A second notion ordered about the temporal consideration of human life is that of the generation. Dilthey admits that he has used this concept before, but without letting the substratum beneath its appearance—which is based on his philosophical

66. Ibid., p. 360.
67. *Die dichterische und philosophische Bewegung in Deutschland* 1770–1800 in *Gesammelte Schriften*, vol. 5, pp. 12–27.

conception of history—become evident.[68] Thus we see that, despite its brevity, the idea of the generation is no mere passing fancy with Dilthey; on the contrary, it arises out of the profound structure of his thought.

What is a generation for Dilthey? Two distinct although related meanings are implied in the term. First, a generation is a span of time, an inner metrical notion of human life. "This period of time lasts from birth until that age when, on the average, a new ring is added to the generational tree, and [it] therefore comprises some thirty years. European intellectual history since Thales, the first scientific investigator whose name and merits have been preserved, comprises only eighty-four generations. Barely fourteen generations separate us from the last flowering of Scholasticism."[69] However—and this is the second meaning—"a generation is also a term applied to a *relationship of contemporaneity between individuals,* that is, between those who in one way or another grew up together, who had a common childhood, a common adolescence, and whose years of greatest manly vigor partially overlap. We say that such men belong to the same generation. Hence the connection between such persons results from a deeper relationship. Those who received the same guiding influences in their formative years jointly constitute a generation. So understood, *a generation is composed of a tightly bound circle of individuals* who are so linked as to form a unit made homogeneous by dependence on the same great events and variations that appeared in their formative age, whatever the diversity of other additional factors."[70]

68. "Although I had indeed made use of the basic idea in my presentation, and this idea underlies my philosophical view of history, at the same time it is not readily apparent" (*Über das Studium* . . . in *Gesammelte Schriften,* vol. 5, p. 36).
69. *Über das Studium,* p. 37.
70. Ibid., p. 37.

In the first of these two meanings Dilthey clings to the genealogical interpretation of the generation and this leads him to fix its duration at thirty years. But notice that the examples of actual generations offered by way of illustration seem to belie this number. All the names of Novalis' generation fall between 1767 and 1775, and it does not seem probable that Dilthey would have agreed to include in it men born during an entire thirty-year period. For otherwise, two of the three generations he discovers in German life at the end of the eighteenth century could be placed within such a period. If out of sheer inertia he holds to the old idea of a genealogical generation, when Dilthey thinks historically about *actual* generations, which appear to him as such because of their make-up, they are based on quite another kind of duration.

As for the second and more important meaning, it is well to remember the following points: 1. Although Dilthey uses the common word "contemporaneity" (*Gleichzeitigkeit*), he is really thinking about what Ortega calls, with conceptual exactitude, "coetaneousness." By this term is meant individuals who not only live at the same time but who also have had the same childhood, the same adolescence—who are, in other words, the same *age*. 2. Dilthey astutely observes, though probably without discovering the underlying reasons, that from this similarity of life experiences there appears an even deeper relationship. 3. He insistently points out a time of "receptiveness" in life. 4. The idea of generation appears as an essential determinant of human life and historical coexistence.

But along with these decisive insights, which lend Dilthey's writings an unparalleled value in the history of this theme, certain radical deficiencies must also be stressed. 1. Dilthey outlines his theory of generations in terms of individual life, or, at the most, of inter-individual coexistence. As he sees it, there are certain vicissitudes that befall individuals, certain relationships or communities occurring among individuals as such. 2. For this reason, he sees a generation as a closed circle of individuals—in short, as a group. When he lists the illustrious names that comprise Novalis' generation, he does not see them *belonging* to that generation; they *are* that generation. At times he speaks more accurately of men "representing" a generation, but this idea is never formally thought out and stated. 3. This serves to explain the importance he attributes to great events and changes affecting the individuals who constitute a generation, and his failure to see that the most crucial factor is the social structure in which such individuals are immersed. Thus, Dilthey's brilliant grasp of the reality of individual human life is weakened by a strange inability to understand collective life. As a result he never discovers the real "setting" of generations and their true nature escapes him.

Leopold von Ranke

It is strange that in this series of attempts to elaborate a theory of generations—a significant historiological concept—we have yet to encounter a professional historian. Now, for the first time, we shall not only meet a historian, but one of the greatest of all time: Leopold von Ranke (1795–1886). In recent decades Germans have been wont to trace the historical doctrine of generations to Ranke. We can now see to what degree this is incorrect. Ranke's contributions are made rather late and are, one must add, so tenuous as to be hardly in existence at all. We discover his contribution to the theme rather more in his personal influence on several disciples who mention him—especially, as we shall see, Ottokar Lorenz.

There is only one often-quoted text in which Ranke explicitly mentions the idea of generations. It is found in a paragraph of the appendix to the definitive edition of his first book, *History of Roman and Germanic Peoples in the Fifteenth and Sixteenth*

Centuries, written in 1824.[71] In this celebrated paragraph he states: "It would perhaps be a worthy task to present, as far as possible, generations one after the other, as they are bound to each other and as they separate on the stage of universal history. Justice would then have to be done to each of them. One might describe a series of illustrious figures, those men who in every generation maintain close relationships and whose antagonisms advance the world's evolution. Events correspond to the nature of such men." This is everything, or almost everything, that Ranke has to say on the subject. He wrote thousands of pages of history in which generations are mentioned not at all. In delving into his writings, I have been able to find only a few sentences that clarify the meaning of the second half of the cited paragraph— and which, of course, would be totally irrelevant without it. They are of value only in showing that Ranke had a long-standing although unexpressed interest in the theme. In the first of several lectures delivered by Ranke in 1854 at Berchtesgaden before King Maximilian II of Bavaria, "On the Periods of Modern History," these scant allusions are found: "In every period of humanity there is manifested a certain great tendency; and progress is based on the fact that in every period a certain movement of the human spirit is apparent, which causes first one tendency and then another, and which is properly discernible in them. Yet should one wish to admit, in contradiction to the opinion herein expressed, that progress consists in the fact that in each succeeding period human life potential increases, and hence that each generation completely outstrips those preceding it, and that the last would always be the most privileged, while those preceding would be merely the foundation of those following, then this

71. Leopold von Ranke, *Geschichte der romanischen und germanischen Völker im 15. und 16. Jahrhundert* (*Sämtliche Werke,* Vol. 33), p. 323.

would be a Divine injustice. Such a generation, subservient as it were to larger ends, would be meaningless in and of itself. Only as a step to the following generation would it have meaning. It would stand in no immediate relationship to the Divine. But this I affirm: every period is immediate to God, and its worth is not measured by what springs from it, but by its very existence, by its own being . . . The notion of the education of human kind certainly contains some truth. Yet *before God all the generations of humanity appear equally justified, and so must the historian also consider things* . . . I believe that *in any generation real moral greatness is the same as in any other,* and that in moral greatness there is no superior power."[72]

The two principal points in Ranke's thought are the idea of the shortcomings in the traditional divisions of history and his critique of progressivism. Over against the subordination of each period to the one following, which ends by draining history of all its content, Ranke affirms the essentiality of each period. The real articulation of the latter is made by the generations, which appear as the subjects of history imbued with justification and moral grandeur.

Still, it is clear that Ranke uses the idea of generation imprecisely, with the vague meaning that the term has in his language. The only record of a "theory" is the report that in conversation he once said that a generation is the ". . . expression of certain ideas that are active in the duration of human life."[73] Neither is there the slightest indication of how such an exposition of history by generations, postulated in 1874, could be done. Ranke seems

72. Leopold von Ranke, *Über die Epochen der neueren Geschichte.* Vorträge dem Könige Maximilian II. von Bayern gehalten. Herausgegeben von Alfred Dove. In *Weltgeschichte,* Vol. 4 (Leipzig, 1910), pp. 529–31 (Marias' italics).

73. In the German: "Ausdruck für gewisse im Menschenalter wirksame Ideen."

to have had, then, a vague inkling of the reality of generations and their rôle in history, but he did not really know what a generation is or how it might go about realizing its mission. It was for this reason, according to Lorenz, that Ranke chose not to discuss the topic and would dismiss it with laughter. Lorenz responded that since his skin was thicker that his teacher's, a generation thicker to be exact, he would have to speak out on the subject. Ranke's caution with professional historians is understandable: they would look unfavorably on such an idea—and did so, in fact, when it was formulated more extensively by his disciple. Ranke did not wish to risk an immature and still inchoate thought, one that could be formulated only with difficulty and one that would incur the hostility of his colleagues and jeopardize his enormous prestige. For theoretical reasons, furthermore, it seems most unlikely that Ranke could have achieved a conceptually sufficient understanding of the topic, and Lorenz confirms this conjecture with his own doctrine. Even so, Ranke's fabulous knowledge of historical material and his probity could have been very valuable in forming an empirical component of the theory.

Ottokar Lorenz

Ottokar Lorenz (1832–1907), almost exactly contemporary with Dilthey, posited the problem of generations with greater scope than Ranke, whose work was his point of departure. Lorenz' contribution to the theme is found principally in a two-volume methodological work: *Die Geschichtswissenschaft in Hauptrichtungen und Aufgaben kritisch erörtert* [The Science of History in its Principal Directions and a Critical Discussion of Problems] (Berlin, 1886), and *Leopold von Ranke, die Generationslehre und der Geschichtsunterricht* [Leopold von Ranke, the Theory of Generations and the Teaching of History] (Berlin, 1891).[74] In these two books, especially the second, the Austrian historian expounds his ideas on the theme. Unfortunately, he mixes them with other ideas that detract seriously from the value of his contribution.

Lorenz cites two sources for his doctrine: Ranke and the French psychologist Théodule A. Ribot. The latter, in his book *L'Hérédité psychologique* [Psychological Heredity] (1872), had called attention to the rôle of heredity in history and to the hereditary transmission of national character from one generation to another. Moreover, Lorenz was himself attracted to genealogical research and even wrote a *Lehrbuch der Genealogie* [Textbook of Genealogy] (1898). While criticizing traditional divisions of history, Lorenz observes that one usually speaks of events and forgets that the real basis for events is men. Events are acts and they must be referred to those who act them out as well as to the conditions under which they arise. Rather than the customary procedure of outlining *a priori* great historical divisions, which are then subdivided, Lorenz proposes the opposite approach: beginning with elementary groupings, he would link these to form larger periods until at last he reaches the great historical divisions. The history of men must be reasserted over the history of ideas. Such a history is possible only through genealogy. Historical man is a product of his genealogy in relationship to the mass of his contemporaries. From this discipline, which is the real foundation of history, is derived the history of ideas, men, and institutions. Now, the immediate outcome of all this is a series of individual genealogies; the

74. Mention is made of Lorenz' ideas in several books, but I have found only one of them adequate: the chapter Mentré devotes to him in *Les générations sociales,* pp. 139–74. The reader will find direct references to the original texts that I was not able to consult for the first edition.

generalization of this law permits the formulation of a doctrine of generations.

"Genealogy," says Lorenz, "is the real future doctrine of historical sciences; the time must come when genealogical research will be the basis of all historiography."[75] But he notes that the "qualitative side of genealogy" (*die qualitative Seite der Genealogie*) will have to be included. He goes on to say that "history attempts to explain the character of generations. In order to proceed here with accuracy, it needs genealogy as a basis for any theory of generations. But since it is impossible to determine genealogically the multitude of men, one is always limited to the genealogy of individuals. Yet a law that is verified in individuals becomes generalized when elevated to the concept of a generation. Finally, in the whole range of historical phenomena, one cannot reckon with genealogies, but only with generations."[76] Lorenz, in citing Rümelin, notes that the latter had overlooked that fact that a generation cannot coincide with governments, but that it can be aware of a *historische Alterswirksamkeit,* a historical effectiveness based on age.

Lorenz holds that the coincidence of historical evolution with genealogical evolution must be demonstrated. In the course of a century there are three generations linked in a true relationship, transmitting their experiences directly to each other, and thus constituting a spiritual, historical unity. Historical evolution is based, then, on the real succession of generations. There are "vigorous" generations which execute great changes. The historian has a double mission: first, to ascertain those persons who lend their name to generations, and secondly, to develop the series of generations that have succeeded each other since an initial one. For this purpose portraits and genealogical trees can

75. Ottokar Lorenz, *Die Geschichtswissenschaft in Hauptrichtungen und Aufgaben kritisch erörtert* (Berlin, 1886), pp. 275–76.
76. Ibid., pp. 276–77.

be used. The problem lies in making groupings of contemporaries and in separating the different generations. As for the beginning point, it is not necessary and implies some arbitrariness, but it is not unjustifiable. Ranke liked to begin with 1515, at the time of the struggles between Charles V and Francis I, and Lorenz imitates him.

Later, however, influenced by the philologist Wilhelm Scherer, Lorenz turns to larger groupings embracing periods of three hundred and six hundred years. Here his figures become absolutely gratuitous, inconsistent, and in fact independent of his basic idea.

Lorenz summarizes his conclusions with four results:

1. The objectively posited temporal measure of all historical events is the century.

2. The century is merely a chronological expression of the mutual spiritual and material belonging of three human generations.

3. For the long series of historical events that are to be investigated, a century would be too small a measure, and three generations too short a time.

4. Therefore, as an immediately superior unit of measure, are presented three hundred and six hundred-year periods—three times three generations and three times six generations.[77]

Lorenz does not formally state what a generation is. He offers the following, emphasizing that it is a provisional definition: ". . . all men of the West who for a third of a century act together."[78] The conceptual immaturity of the definition is obvious: the problem is presented in genealogical terms, and for that reason a generation is defined as a plurality of individuals.

77. Ibid., p. 299.
78. In the German: "Die Summe der Menschen, die im Zeitraum eines Drittel-Jahrhunderts gemeinsam im Abenlande wirken."

He accepts the thirty three-year period, traditional in genealogy, but says absolutely nothing as to which third of the century is meant. Nor does he elaborate on the series of the successive thirds. Finally, his restriction of the scheme to the West appears arbitrary and is linked to certain objections that were raised against his theory.

The principal objections were made by Bernheim in the third and fourth editions of the *Lehrbuch der historischen Methode* [Textbook of the Historical Method]. Aroused by previous hostility to all absolute division of history, Bernheim is especially insistent about long periods, which to him seem unjustified and numerical sleight of hand, just as they would later appear to be purely cabalistic to Ernst Troeltsch. But we have already seen that such long periods are neither the only nor the essential portion of Lorenz's doctrine. Bernheim's objections are particularly as follows: (1) If the law of generations is a historical law, it must needs be universal. Since Lorenz restricts it to monogamous peoples, then only such peoples are historical or the law is not historical. (2) Lorenz bases his notion of generations on heredity and calls what is not explained by heredity "the rest." Thus the unknown creative novelty of the individual is admitted.[79] Now, either individual impulses scarcely influence the chain of events, or the theory of generations is not a general principle of historical division. As we shall see, both Lorenz's doctrine and Bernheim's attacks on it painfully reveal the falseness of their common postulates and their ignorance of a generation's "ontological" setting and of the kind of reality it encloses.

Ignaz Jastrow objected to Lorenz's idea of the continuity of births and therefore to the indefinite intermingling of generations. Lorenz responds to this, but again he accepts in principle

79. In the German: "Das neue unbekannte Schöpferische im individuum."

the presupposition behind the objection: that generations consist primarily of individuals who are being born every moment. Indeed, Lorenz questions whether, as one assumes a beginning point, one has the right to omit the millions of real juxtaposed generations and reduce them all to one. But he notes that one generation is separated from another not by a mathematical date but rather by the advent and disappearance of the ideas and designs of men.

In spite of these obscure points, Lorenz has a great deal of confidence in his doctrine of generations: "Within fifty years," he says, "any schoolboy will be as accustomed to this measure (generational calculation) as he is not to the meter."[80] This expectation, as Petersen ironically observes, would be fulfilled only in the case of Lorenz's own son Alfred, who wrote a history of music according to the rhythm of generations.[81] But Petersen fails to see that while it is true that Lorenz's expectation was inordinate, owing to theoretical inconsistencies in his idea of generations (inconsistencies are no means lacking in Petersen's own theory), this does not imply unfruitfulness in the theory itself, once it has been discovered and formulated.

Contributions of the Nineteenth Century

The foregoing are the initial stages of the generational thinking of the nineteenth century. They are few, admittedly, but not so few as many suppose. But what did they accomplish? At this point we must seek to attain a balanced view of what the nineteenth century knew about the generations theme. The first men to study the problem scientifically were astute, ingenious,

80. In the German: "Im 50 Jahren wird jeder Schulknabe mit diesem Masstab (die Generations rechnung) ebenso geläufig umgehen, wie er heute mit dem Meter verfährt."
81. Alfred Lorenz, *Abenländische Musikgeschichte im Rhythmus der Generationen* (Berlin, 1928).

full of intellectual interest. In the worst cases this "interest" assumed the deficient, though hardly despicable, form of mere curiosity. There is an essential difference between approaching problems out of theoretical necessity or while coming to grips with reality, and approaching these same problems only because they are stylish or the current topic of conversation. When later we examine the attempts made in this century to master the generations theme, we shall encounter, all too often, not the sincerity and originality of eighty or a hundred years ago but a certain frivolity and a lack of intellectual maturity. This necessarily implies a lack of information and, even more significantly, a lack of conceptual precision.

What, then, did the nineteenth century know about generations? It can be summarized briefly as follows:

1. The mechanism of historical change by generations (Comte). The influence of the biological component (longevity) by its repercussion on the structure of society and on the rhythm of conservative and innovative tendencies.

2. The idea of generations as ". . . sets of human beings that take possession of society" (Mill). The historicity of generations; the total character of each of them (*consensus*) as a form of life. The historical, rather than biological or simply static sociological, nature of the *content* of each generation (also Mill).

3. The duration of a generation as a fifteen-year period discovered empirically (Soulavie, Dromel, Benloew). The absence of a theory concerning this point and the lack of sufficient experience (Comte, Mill) as well as partial theories (Lorenz, Dilthey himself) lead to the traditional idea of a thirty-year generation. In Dilthey this inherited genealogical concept is at odds with the chronology of his specific examples.

4. An outline of the *structure* of the generation (Dilthey) as an essential determinant of human life and coexistence.

We can never fully understand the significance of what is

known unless we also take note of what we know is not known, superimposing the one set of facts on the other in order to arrive at a just point of view. This being so, we must ask: what do we know that the nineteenth century did *not* know about generations?

1. First of all, and paradoxical as it may sound, the nineteenth century was quite unaware of all that I have said it "knew." What I have summarized in a few lines—and expounded earlier in greater detail—*no one really knew*. The first theorists on the subject of the generations, and even more so the theorists who come later, were unaware of each other. No one gathered together the scattered bits of information that the various writers were acquiring. Reducing the point to its simplest terms, it is enough to state that the two most valuable contributions to the theory of generations—the idea of interpreting them in terms of a concept of society (Comte and Mill) and the idea of interpreting them in terms of a concept of human life (Dilthey)—arose independently, without any apparent reference to each other.

2. The "setting" of generations. Except for Dromel and Ferrari, all the theorists surveyed fell into the genealogical error, and even the two exceptions had no clear notion of the problem since they reduced the setting to political life alone.

3. The reality of the generation. Generational reality was confused with individual reality or with certain statistical findings. The idea of *vigencia* (prevailing social customs or laws)— the decisive factor, as we shall see later on—was missing.

4. The dynamic relationship between masses and minorities.

5. The contemporaneity–coetaneity relationship and the real articulation of generations.

In summary, there was no theory of generations in the nineteenth century, and there could be none because there was no adequate theory of historical and social life in general—the "setting" of generations. For lack of an adequate concept of human life, there could be only partial anticipations of a theory of generations to the extent that Comte was able to construct a theory of society and Dilthey an idea of human life (notwith-standing the latter's strange inability to understand collective life). The theory of generations, in the full meaning of the term, was simply not yet possible. Once it became a possibility, it was not long in becoming an actuality.

3

Ortega's
Theory of Generations

WE HAVE SEEN THAT IN THE NINETEENTH CENTURY
there was not—there could not be—a theory of generations in the
full meaning of the term. For such a theory to be possible, philosophy had to take certain decisive steps toward establishing the
basic postulates, and it is only in the present century that these
steps have been taken. But almost as soon as the theory was a
possibility, it was indeed formulated—possibly without so much
as a year's delay. This strange precociousness cannot but cause us
to suspect that the development of the theory was a matter of
necessity, for the early germination of an idea is usually an
indication that it is urgently needed to meet some intellectual,
and in general, historical, situation.

The first theory of generations worthy of the name is that
of Ortega. However, it would be a mistake to think that Ortega
has an independent and autonomous doctrine concerning generations, or that it forms in his thought an isolated intellectual unity
that one can simply accept or reject. His doctrine on the generations had to arise out of a general theory of social and historical
reality, and it forms, in turn, an indispensable element of that
reality. Further, the generation theory is rooted in a systematic
conception of reality as such—in a metaphysics. One should not

forget that the philosopher, strictly speaking, does not have "ideas," much less flashes of genius; what are commonly understood to be such are only the ingredients or moments of a superior systematic totality, with which they have a strict and necessary relationship. The philosophy of Ortega is especially systematic, for this characteristic of his thought is based not on a deliberate attempt at systematization, but rather on the discovery that reality is itself systematic. In this kind of situation, the philosopher is systematic whether he wants to be or not.

Therefore, Ortega's theory of generations cannot be considered as an isolated segment of his work. If at times it is supposed that he usually presented his theory in this way—that is, isolated in substance from his basic assumptions—the misunderstanding must be taken as an indication of some curious intellectual habits of our time. The first mature and explicit formulation of Ortega's generation theory is found in the chapter, entitled "The Idea of Generations," of his *El tema de nuestro tiempo* [The Modern Theme], which is to say in the book that constitutes the first formal presentation of his philosophy as a whole. This being so, how is it possible not to realize at once that this theory is an essential ingredient of his philosophical system? Are we to imagine that this first chapter is there by pure happenstance, or because he jumbled the pages of the manuscript?

It is necessary, then, to refer to Ortega's philosophy at this point, but only inasmuch as his historical and social theory is derived from it. And as for the social theory, it must have our attention only insofar as it reveals the place where the concrete theory of generations is lodged—its location on the intellectual map of reality, as it were. For these reasons, we propose to trace hurriedly and only in outline an incomplete and undetailed map of Ortega's thought, in order to be able later to locate the more exactly and minutely drawn chart of our promised land.[1]

1. In other books I have explained Ortega's philosophy either in depth or in outline, and the reader desiring to go deeper into

Metaphysical Foundations

Ortega's philosophical innovation is of a very precise order of magnitude, and not at all unrelated to the possibility of a theory of generations. Any metaphysics is a certain idea of reality, and each metaphysical system is distinguished from others by its discovering and exploring a new reality, or by its considering reality from a new perspective and thereby revealing hitherto unknown dimensions. But there are moments in the history of thought when a greater change is needed. In such times it is not enough merely to integrate a previous vision of reality with that produced by other portions or aspects of the same, previously ignored or unknown. Rather, the meaning of reality itself is brought into question. Stated in another way, the problem ceases to be one of identifying the primary or most important realities and becomes one of determining, regardless of what those primary *realities* may be, what *reality* itself is. This problem, that of seeking to know what it means "to be reality," is a far more serious matter than distinguishing between the primary and secondary aspects of reality. When the very meaning of reality itself is brought into question, philosophy undergoes a decisive inflection and begins one of its notable periods, one of the great articulations of its history.

We are not attempting here an evaluation of Ortega's work, but rather a true characterization of the historical significance of his thought. For it must be admitted that the decisive inflections of philosophy are not due simply to the workings of genius,

---

his thought may consult these works. An abbreviated explanation is found in my *Historia de la Filosofía* (*Obras*, I). Several studies are included in *La escuela de Madrid* (*Obras*, V); and a detailed commentary on *Meditaciones del Quijote* is found in the version of this book by the University of Puerto Rico (Revista de Occidente, 1957). Above all, see my book *Ortega 1. Circunstancia y vocación* (Madrid: Revista de Occidente, 1960).

though genius is doubtless necessary to bring them about. Rather, they are demanded and postulated by the very situation to which man has arrived. Hence the entire age preludes, announces, and attempts them. Moreover, it is not always possible to formulate, fully and with philosophical maturity, the new idea as it appears on the historical scene in response to a change of situation. One has only to imagine how far we are from achieving an adequate philosophical elaboration—and with it a clarification of intellectual possibilities—of the idea of reality revealed in the situation defined by Christianity. In all these centuries, the real possibilities of this situation have either been freely and authentically revealed to only a very slight extent or they have been obscured by disturbing extraneous factors.

Now, Ortega is found in the very center of one of these modifications. Leaving aside the question of how successful he has been in reaching a new idea of reality—this is, in fact, a task of several generations, and the decision as to his genius must await the future—clearly the unmistakable and precise discovery of that reality can be traced to him.

Radical reality, that reality in which all others, regardless of their nature and location, are rooted or from which they arise, is our life. Realism and idealism, strictly speaking, spring from a common idea of reality, and come into opposition with each other only in regard to the priority of certain realities over others. To be reality for one and the other is *to be a thing,* whether the primary reality is what we call "things" or *res,* or whether it is that thing we call "I" (*res cogitans*). When Ortega says that radical reality is neither the "I" nor "things" but life, he is not proposing some third "thing" but something that is not a "thing" at all. Stated in other words, he transcends the idea of reality that was the common supposition of realism and idealism and gives a new meaning to the expression "to be real."

To state that radical reality is our life, that of each one, may appear to be a theory; but this is precisely what it is not! It is not a theory, true or false, but a simple statement of fact. For life is that within which we find ourselves, regardless of what we may otherwise wish, after we have rejected all theories. *Living consists of what we do and of what happens to us.* This is in no way a theory but simply reality as I find it.

But what is it that I find? I find myself with *things,* surrounded by them: I and the things around me. If we latinize this, we may say that life is I and my circumstance. Is it then a matter of the sum of two parts, that is, I and the things around me? Not at all, because the basic fact is life, which is what I am doing with things. To live is to busy oneself continuously with things, to have to be inexorably doing something with them; and what I do, what I create, is precisely my life. *Life is given me, but it is not given to me ready-made.* One fine day I found myself living —without anyone having consulted me about it—and ever since I have had to be doing something all the time, one thing or another, in order to live. Life is presented to me as an unavoidable task. The decisive element, therefore, is neither things nor I, both of which are partial and abstract ingredients of my life, but rather what I *do* with things. The important fact is the drama, complete with characters, plot, and stage-setting, which I call "my life."

This task is imposed on me by circumstance, which means a repertory of facilities and difficulties, the source of my possibilities and at the same time an awesome limitation. But circumstance neither decides nor defines my life, restrict it though it may. It is I who must decide at every instant to do one thing or another; I must at all times choose my way from among my possibilities. To do this I need a plan of life, a vital project, a more or less vague image of the direction of my life; I must have a goal that lends form to my life. This plan is what causes me at each moment to decide among my possibilities, to choose one and postpone others. This means that at every moment in order to decide, in order to shape my life, I must justify—first of all to myself—why I do one thing and not some other. Life is inherently responsibility just as it is intrinsically moral. Morality is neither a veneer nor a luxuriant or convenient supplement to life but rather its unappealable condition. Every act, and therefore the totality of life, is necessarily moral, which is to say moral or immoral. Man is perforce *free* because he can at no time cease to select and to decide for himself. No one else can do this for him. The only freedom that man does *not* have is the freedom to stop being free, to renounce his freedom.

If human life is "no-thing"—not a material thing like those of the physical world, nor a "thinking thing," nor even that quasi-thing of doubtful nature called an idea—then we are dealing with a peculiar and distinct reality. While things have a being already bestowed and fixed, human life is essentially incomplete, and man must not only complete the life given him: he must also imagine and invent it before he can finish it. This is what Ortega means by his repeated assertion that life is a poetic task. Man is a plastic reality. This does not mean, of course, that his is an unlimited plasticity, but it does imply that it is indefinite, especially if we consider man in general rather than individually. Man cannot be anything he likes; he can and indeed has to imagine and decide what he will be. This is more crucial than it may seem at first. In a certain sense man's existence is determined by what is called "nature": he is a terrestial animal of certain proportions, he breathes through lungs and is subject to biological conditions that he cannot escape—he cannot, let us say, decide to be the size of a microbe or ten miles tall. Yet strictly speaking, is even this as impossible as it appears? To be the size of bacteria means to be able to operate at this level of magnitude, and man has been able to do this by inventing the electron microscope. By means of stratospheric airplanes he multiplies his

height by ten thousand and thereby surmounts his biological
limitations in a most real and effective way. As I noted earlier, in
an overlooked portion of his work Comte spoke of the
". . . positive theory of social alterability," hardly guessing the
profound meaning of his words. The time to discover the brilliant depth of this idea is at hand.

Human life with its singular plastic nature is the setting or
area where reality as such is constituted. Reality is what in one
way or another appears within my life, although this reality may
assume the form of exceeding or transcending it. It may even be
the cause of my life. Within my life there is formed the characteristic of being real, the *realitas* of that which is real, and which
may, in fact, transcend life in every way. In life is found even
that peculiar form of reality which is the unreality of impossibilities such as the squared circle or the unextended color. Such
"realities" are "rooted" in life without being in it, since in an
absolute sense they are nowhere to be found.

When certain men in the nineteenth century began to have
glimpses of the changing and unstable reality that is human life,
they felt as though they were losing their footing. The instrument of Reason, which they had hitherto used to learn of things,
became unsuitable for the task. This was the beginning of irrationalism, which surreptitiously is evident for the rest of the
century, from the time of Kierkegaard until it truly flourishes
during the last decades of that century and the first years of our
own in such men as William James, Bergson, Unamuno, and
Spengler. In different ways these writers all say that mere intelli-
gence does not comprehend life. Reason, which fixes and solidi-
fies everything it touches, cannot grasp the living, the unstable,
the moving. To accept the concrete reality of human life or
existence is, then, to fall into irrationalism. But one must not
forget that this notion was most widely believed between 1880
and 1910. It is not a current philosophy. Hence when existential-

ism for the most part falls back into the irrational attitude, it is only repeating what others thought many years ago in response to a situation quite different than ours. On the other hand, what is usually offered in opposition to this philosophy is a kind of rationalism whose deficiencies and outright impossibilities, once recognized as such, provoke a return to the irrationalism of the past century. In other words, the very cause of that old irrationalism, and what partially justified it in the first place, is being revived and proposed as an alternative to irrationalism! Only now—and this time in Spain first—have we surpassed both irrationalism and the assumptions that made it possible.

What was understood by "reason" in the last third of the nineteenth century was abstract or "pure" reason, which attempts to view things in an essential immutability, *sub specie aeterni.* But *life* is a continuing flux; it is subject to fundamental change and at every instant is in the process of creating itself; it is never the same from one instant to the next. How, then, is it possible to know life? Over against *abstract* or *pure* reason, as successful in mathematics and physics as it is unsuccessful in the sciences dealing with man, one must turn to *vital* reason, that is, living reason. This reason is faithful to the perspective in which man finds himself at any given moment and is amenable to the essential mobility of life. This habit of gratuitously attributing eternity to things not only makes it harder to comprehend them but also obscures the idea of the Divinity itself.

"Vital reason," as I have written elsewhere and should like to quote here, *"is life itself, one and the same thing as living.* What does this mean? Its meaning becomes clearer if we consider another statement: *to live is to have no other recourse than to reason in the face of inexorable circumstance.* Since life is not complete, but rather something that must be completed, and since we at every moment must choose from among the possibilities offered by our situation, we need to be fully aware of this condition in its entirety. This is what is meant here by 'reason.' Therefore, because he does not have a prefabricated being, man cannot live without orienting himself, that is, without thinking or reasoning. Hence life in its very substance is reason. But when we look at things from the other side, to understand is to know what to rely on regarding one's situation. In other words, a thing is understood when it functions within my life in its circumstantial entirety. This means that reason—the instrument that allows us to comprehend reality—is nothing other than life itself. This is the meaning of 'vital reason': the reason of life, or with greater accuracy, the reason that is life. The expression *living reason* which Ortega also used is clearer concerning this radical complication of reason and human life. It is life in its actual movement, in its biographical manifestation; it is what lends understanding and meaning to things."[2] But let us not think only nor even particularly of overly complicated things. To understand the smallest and humblest reality—for instance, what we usually call "a glass of water"—is to cause it to function within my life. It becomes something subject to diverse acts on my part that cause it to assume different functions, which is to say, different realities. I refer to this "something" as a glass because I usually drink from it; yet I could place it in the pan of a balance and convert it into a weight. Hurled at my enemy, it becomes a projectile. I could sell it and thus change it into an item of merchandise, or break it and use the pieces as a cutting instrument. I could pretend to foretell the future by looking at the reflections in it, as the Count of Cagliostro did. From this apparently singular reality that we call—a bit hastily it would seem—"a glass of water," many other realities have started to proliferate that are understandable *only* insofar as my life reveals their meaning.

2. "Ortega y la idea de la razón vital," *La escuela de Madrid* (*Obras,* V), pp. 328–29.

Human things are understood only when their story is told, when what has happened is made known. We can only begin to understand a man when we learn what he has done previously in view of his circumstance and his plan of life. Since man is not an isolated being but one who lives in a society, and since society is historical, the whole of history weighs on every human act. We must appeal, therefore, to history in its entirety, since it has happened to each of us. This means that the concrete form of vital or living reason is *historical* reason. But keep in mind that this historical and vital reason is not a *particular* form of Reason, but rather the contrary: it is reason unmodified and without adjectives, reason in the fullest sense, as opposed to the abstract particularizations and simplifications of reason. The latter are usually confused with reason because these imperfect forms are the only ones about which theories have been formulated up to now. In order to understand mathematical and physical realities (which are not realities in the strictest sense) abstract, pure, physico-mathematical, geometrical reason—whatever one may wish to call it—is *perhaps* enough. But such reason is certainly not enough to live by. Living calls for a superior and more complex reason: vital reason or, if one prefers, historical reason.

This means, therefore, that we are dealing with a "narrative" reason. But it should be pointed out that any concrete narration presupposes an abstract analysis. Human life and history cannot be understood in their real manifestation without the unreal and a priori component of analysis or abstract theory of life, which are universal and necessary but take on a definite character only when they are circumstantialized. This means that such universal theses have a functional nature; they are *leere Stellen* or "empty places" destined to be "filled," to acquire meaningful form as they assume a circumstantial and historical existence. We shall see later how this formal sketch becomes clearer in the particular case of the theory of generations.[3]

Historical and Social Life

In its first and fullest sense, human life is always individual life: it is my life, yours, or someone else's. Yet within my life, and as a part of it, I discover the lives of others. To live is something that happens in the form of coexistence. Coexistence is previous to the two forms it may assume, presence or company and absence or loneliness, for loneliness is loneliness *from others.*

But here the problems begin. Sociologists have tried to make a theory of social or collective life and in so doing they have countervailed it against individual life. Even the most astute of them have thought that the coexistence of several individuals is all that is needed to have a society. On the one hand stands the individual, on the other, social or collective reality. But they have overlooked something very important, something which Ortega points out, and which hitherto has led to the confusion that has invalidated the otherwise admirable efforts of contemporary sociologists. What Ortega discovers is "interindividual" reality—the reality, the relationships, between several individuals acting as individuals. So long as there are merely individuals as such (regardless of their number), there are only individual life and interindividual relationships. Nowhere is social or collective reality apparent. Moreover, society has been interpreted repeatedly as "association," as something predated by individual life. Society has been seen as the result of willful actions on the part of individuals. Yet this interpretation does not take into account the fact that society is something that simply *is there;* it is something

3. For a treatment of all these problems, see my *Introducción a la Filosofía,* especially Chapter 5, "La razón" (*Obras,* II).

in which the individual finds himself and which has nothing to do with his will or any personal act of association. For Simmel, ". . . society exists wherever several individuals enter into a reciprocal action . . . ; this reciprocal action is always produced by certain instincts or for certain ends."[4] This implies that individuals are previous to society. These individuals, by means of a personal act, "enter" into society and their doing this is enough to assure the existence of society. Finally, society presupposes some "end," whether instinctive or deliberately sought. For Weber, in turn, ". . . social action . . . is guided by the actions of others. . . ." These " 'others' can be individualized and known or a plurality of undetermined and completely unknown individuals."[5] This means that in Weber's view, also, for society to exist it is enough to have an interaction directed by the reciprocal conduct of individuals. This view formally excludes the distinction between the interindividual and the social, with the immediately obvious result that both things are confused.

The interindividual, then, is not identified with the individual *sensu stricto,* and is identified even less with the social. Three rather than two categories must be pointed out: the individual, individuals, and society. The social is manifested in the form of "usages": what is said, what is believed, what is done. In other words, this is what *people* say, believe, or do; and by people is meant anybody and consequently nobody in particular—no individual in the sense of a personal individual. Society is impersonal; its contents and dictates are imposed on its individual members regardless of personal opinion and will. The motives behind social actions are not personal but arise from the automatic efficacy of the social body and from the system of reprisals

4. Georg Simmel, *Sociología* (Spanish translation, Revista de Occidente, 1926), I, p. 15.
5. Max Weber, *Economía y Sociedad* (Spanish translation, Fondo de Cultura Económica, Mexico, 1944), I, p. 4.

brought to bear on those who fail to comply with its usages. Nobody greets another person, dresses in a certain way, or eats according to a fixed routine because he *personally* thinks such things should be done. He does them this way because that is "what is done." And since belonging to society is not a voluntary choice but the result of man finding himself in a society regardless of his likes and dislikes, and since man cannot enlist in or resign from the fact of being born into a certain family in a certain country (as he might from an association of fishermen or chess players), man finds himself decisively affected and conditioned by the repertory of social usages that constrain and oppress him, that regulate his behavior but which at the same time, by virtue of their automatic nature, resolve and decide a great portion of his life. Furthermore, what we call society is not a static or even stable reality but a dynamic, problematic resultant of the forces of sociation and dissociation.

The decisive idea is that of *vigencia,* or binding custom, which we shall see reappear many times in this book.[6] Social usages, beliefs, and current ideas are imposed on individuals automatically. Individuals find themselves living in the midst of usages with their impersonal and anonymous pressure. This does not mean that the individual must necessarily yield to the demands of current customs, but he does have to be aware of them; he must confront them in order to accept or reject them. This is what it means for a social usage to be prevalent and enforced.

6. *Vigencia* was originally a legal term and referred principally to laws and practices current and in force. Ortega and Marías use the term to describe laws, customs, usages, traditions, and beliefs that currently prevail in a given society or collectivity. *Vigencia* is related to that which has life (*quod viget*). They are social forces arising from many sectors of life and imposed on us without the intervention of our will. They are binding, impersonal forces that form the very fabric of the collectivity [translator's note].

Each of us must create his life within a world defined by a system of such prevailing usages. We must give an account of what we are doing by taking into account the sum total of the ingredients of the world in which we find ourselves. In this life we have at our disposal a limited time with a finite horizon—our days are numbered—and, as we saw earlier, the time we have is qualified by age, so that the years we have are not only few; they are unexchangeable. If the span of human life can be imagined as a sum of spendable money that can be enjoyed until it is gone, then the mismanaged investment can be looked on as a conclusive loss. But the comparison is still somewhat inaccurate, for money is uniformly the same and if one investment fails I can still make another—though perhaps at the cost of having to forego others. But time is not the same as money. A closer parallel would be ration coupons, which are not only limited as to quantity but are restricted to certain products and are thus untransferable. If one uses up his clothing coupons, he may not buy more clothing by sacrificing food coupons. In the same way, the years of a wasted youth are irreplaceable and may not be compensated for by others later; the other years of life are inexorably different, years of maturity or old age with their own peculiar possibilities and limitations.

Life, which is not given to us complete, is difficult. It can be turned to good or evil. I can do that for which I truly feel a calling or I can be unfaithful to my vocation and falsify my life. Not all vocations are possible in any given period; for instance, it is unlikely that anyone today feels a calling to be a Knight Templar. But if the distances are shortened, it becomes possible to have anachronisms of vocation and with it a coefficient of automatic inauthenticity. At this point the problem of today, of the historical present, reappears. Because at this very date children playing their first games coexist with elderly scholars born in the time of Isabel II (queen of Spain, 1833–1868).

Man is in the world, *each person* is also in *his* world. Each has his own circumstances and these are different in each case, though a certain correspondence between them may be possible. First of all, each man's historical world is his generation, and from it he must face reality in order to mold his life. Seen within this context, generations acquire an unexpected dramatic appearance. For our generation is a fundamental ingredient of each of us. I cannot live of and by myself; willy nilly, I live only within my generation. This being so, it becomes an urgent and vital problem to be able to distinguish generations! Far from being a leisurely intellectual entertainment, a matter of curiosity, the problem concerns each of us personally. Always, in speaking of things human, we may repeat with the Latin: *de te fabula narratur* [the story is about you].

Chronology of the Theme

The foregoing postulates are necessary for an understanding of Ortega's theory of generations. So far as I know, this is the first time they have been set forth specifically as a prelude to an exposition of his ideas on the topic, and yet it seems that without them it is not possible to understand the necessity, the intellectual justification, the true content, or the scope of the theory.

Now, before expounding on Ortega's theory of generations as such, we must raise the question of when he began to busy himself with the theme. In matters of history, chronology is especially important—not, as once was the custom, as an external accessory or superfluous bit of detail but as an indispensable part of understanding itself. We have already remarked that today the first thing we need to ascertain in order to understand something is *when* it was done or said. But how accurate need this information be? Is it absolutely necessary for us to stuff our memory and books with exact dates? There appears to be no other alternative, at least for the moment, given the fact that what I have called the elemental historical present has become questionable and we feel lost in the flow of time. Yet as soon as a satisfactory theory of generations is formulated and the real process of generational change is sufficiently determined, it will only be necessary to appoint each event to a particular generation. When this happens, this inferior mathematical exactness will give way to a superior historical accuracy; dates will have lost their abstract numerical character and instead will express rigorous human realities.

Before proceeding it would be well to enumerate the dates and works in the published writings of Ortega in which the theory of generations has appeared and been formulated over a period of time:[7]

1914: *Vieja y nueva política* [Old and New Politics]. First mention is made of his awareness of the generation. In the same year *Meditaciones del Quijote* [Meditations on Quixote] appears; it is the first conceptual formulation of Ortega's philosophy (*Obras,* I, pp. 270, 271, 307).

1917: In any period three generations coexist. The men of the Republic, the Restoration, and Ortega's generation are living at the same time. The distinction is made between "contemporaneity" and "coetaneity": between living at the same time and being the same age (*Obras,* III, p. 12).

1922: At a banquet, in "The Sacred Crypt of Pombo," Ortega with great preciseness refers to the generation as ". . . the most important concept of history," and points out the generational mechanism (*Obras,* III, p. 12).

1923: *El tema de nuestro tiempo* [*The Modern Theme*]. In this the first formal presentation of his theory—the book is a

7. All references are to José Ortega y Gasset's *Obras completas,* 6 vols. (Madrid: *Revista de Occidente,* 1946–47). The only exception is the last reference.

development of a lesson given in 1921—a series of decisive concepts appears: mass and minority, vital sensitivity, historical life as coexistence, the generation as a human variety, vital level, pulsation, vocation, the true mission of each generation, coetaneity, and metahistory (*Obras,* III, pp. 145–52, 163).

1924: An allusion is made to generations as human harvests and to the mutations that appear in them (*Obras,* III, p. 268).

1925: Again he mentions "three generations that coexist at any historical date." He describes a system of assumptions prevailing at any period and differing among these contemporary generations. He speaks of understanding and misunderstanding among them (*Obras,* III, p. 424).

1926: A disturbing theme appears: woman. Ortega discusses amorous relationships within and without the generation, as well as the problem of synchronism of the sexes in generations. He describes generations as caravans within which each individual journeys and is by chance together with others for a limited time. He refers to the generation as ". . . a complete way of life that imprints itself indelibly on the individual" (*Obras,* III, pp. 439–42).

1930: He discusses limitation, change, and crisis in generations. Mention is made of the three "todays" of each today. Again he brings up contemporaneity and coetaneity. He finds the cause of historical change in the articulation of three generations in any so-called "present." He points out the essential anachronism of history (*Obras,* IV, pp. 89–93).

1930: Ortega speaks of the fifteen-year period of predominance of a generation. The active participation of a generation lasts for thirty years, with two fifteen-year periods: I, a struggle to impose its ideas, preferences, and tastes; and II, the years of dominance and defense against the following generation (*Obras,* IV, pp. 204–5).

1930: He points out a fifteen-year lapse in two phases as being the normal duration of the ". . . inexorable anachronism of imitative and unauthentic peoples" (*Obras*, IV, p. 317).

1933: In *En torno a Galileo* [*Man and Crisis*] we find the general theory of generations in its mature form. The following treatment will refer in particular to these pages (*Obras*, V, pp. 29–71).

1934: Ortega offers a concrete example of the fifteen-year duration of generations. He cites Tacitus: *per quindecim annos, grande mortalis aevi spatium* (Fifteen years is a long time in human life) (*Obras*, III, p. 43).

1934: Ortega speaks of innovation on the part of generations; he discusses continuity and discontinuity in history, and generational communication and incommunicability (*Obras*, V, pp. 182–83).

1935: Spanish and French Romantic generations are discussed (*Obras*, V, pp. 243–44).

1940: Ortega refines his theory of generations with the following ideas: a way of life that lasts for a given period, the zone of generational dates, and the unity of authentic historical chronology (*Obras*, VI, pp. 370–75).

1942: He writes of generations as "historical matter" (*Obras*, VI, p. 391).

1943: Ortega's work on *Velázquez*. In this writing, first published in German with an introduction by Ortega in that language, he applies the idea of generation to Velázquez. The work was published in Spanish in 1950, under the title: *Papeles sobre Velázquez y Goya* [Papers on Velázquez and Goya] (later included in his *Obras Completas*, VIII, pp. 453–660).

This detailed chronology of the theme will make it unnecessary for me to make repeated references to it in the following pages. We can see how Ortega was concerned with the generation throughout his intellectual life. His two principal presentations of the concept are *The Modern Theme* (1923) and *Man and Crisis* (1933). The dates of the appearance of most of his basic and attendant ideas are given. With this we may proceed to present the theory in a systematic form. The reader will be able to check the texts by referring to the chronology given above.

The Analytical Theory of Generations

We must try to clarify the portion of the doctrine of generations that is derived from a sufficient analysis of human, individual, and collective life. This analysis is what we earlier called an abstract or analytical theory, and it leaves untouched for the moment a second question of perhaps greater difficulty: the empirical existence of generations and the way of determining their succession, or at least the method for doing so. We can, in fact, know *a priori* and by pure analysis both the nature of generations and the fact that they exist. Only a very complex historical inquiry would permit us to ascertain which generations are the real ones.

Our point of departure has been a summary analysis of human life as Ortega thought it to be. We saw that life, properly speaking, does not consist of the psychophysical elements of man —his body and soul—but of what man does with these elements. That which is truly human is not the somatic or psychic apparatus or instruments with which man is endowed, and it is not the immediate circumstance in which he finds himself and to which he is forever linked; life is what man *does* with the whole of his circumstance, the *purposes* to which he puts his psychophysical, natural, social, and historical world. Life is a play, complete with actor, plot, and stage setting. It consists of what each of us makes of himself and his circumstance, after having planned or imagined his life from the possibilities of his world.

This and *only* this is the promising point of departure in an effort to discover the nature of human generations. Any point of

view based on biology—for example, any genealogical consideration—misses the point. For the biological is only an ingredient or
component—and as such an abstraction—of human life, and the
authentic reality of life lies beyond it.

Each of us lives in a world. If we were asked what "world"
means, we should have to answer that in an immediate and
provisional sense "world" is a system of compulsory usages (*vigencias*). This reply may seem somewhat strange, and more
so if it is supposed that the world is an aggregate of "things." It
may even be affirmed, and not without a certain petulance, that
the world is not, and cannot be, more than this. But if we press
the matter further, we must ask ourselves: what are "things"? If
we look about us we find many of them indeed, yet it is problematic why we consider these entities to be things, why we call a
certain portion of matter a thing—not something more or less
—and thus set it apart with a certain distinctness from the
totality of the world. Any appeal to physical unity is insufficient,
since a thing—a glass, a stone, or anything else—is physically
composed of another type of separate unities called molecules;
these in turn are made of atoms, atoms of protons, electrons,
neutrons, and so on. Why do we group certain combinations of
these particles into a unit that we label a thing? Why this
combination and not others? Our mere relative size and the
quantitative nature of our sense organs determine such groupings. For us a stone is a thing, but the dust particles comprising
the stone are not. However, viewed under a microscope the stone
would dissolve into a multitude of independent "things": each
dust particle would become a thing. Likewise, seen from another
planet, the great boulders of our mountain ranges would be
merely integrated elements of other "things" that appear to us as
great and exceedingly complex aggregates. Hence it is immediately apparent that "things" are our *interpretations* of reality. A
radiance in the heavens is interpreted by us today as a physical

phenomenon, by the savage tribesman as an omen, by an ancient Greek as a sign of the wrath of Zeus. Is the radiance one of these three "things," or all three, or none of them?

"The reality 'cat,' " I have remarked elsewhere, "is rigorously different to me, to a mouse, to a flea embedded in his fur, and to a parasite among his intestinal fauna. A possible cat that would be one and the same in all cases is a convention; in the strictest sense, it is a theory or interpretation based on the multiple reality of "cat." Without forcing the point or going beyond human life, we saw that thunder and lightning are different for men of different historical backgrounds. In my own case, a river is something that slakes my thirst, that blocks my way, or is my defense if it is between me and an enemy. These are three distinct vital realities on which I may base my interpretation and which result in the *concept* of a river. Now, this concept may be the only one possible, but it is nonetheless a new element that I use to manipulate other realities. It has never occurred to anybody to confuse a concept of a river, although *in genere* concepts are perhaps mistaken for reality."[8]

The time came when men, having arrived at an interpretation, assumed this interpretation to be reality itself. Reality is thus covered by a patina of interpretations—and reality itself demands them. For to live is to interpret. Any act of life is an interpretation. In order to do something with a thing, I must interpret it as being a certain thing. To walk is to interpret the ground as resistant; if I sow it with seed, I interpret it as the origin of vegetation. To navigate is to interpret water as a road, but if I seek to escape it, I interpret it as a danger, if I drink it from a glass it becomes something that quenches my thirst, if I analyze it in a laboratory I think of it as a chemical substance.

---

8. Marías, *Introducción*, p. 34 (Chapter 3). For this problem, see Chapters 3 and 4.

Yet these interpretations are not mine; they do not originate with me. I have done no more than discover that things are understood in a certain way, that a certain entity was already being interpreted in such and such ways long before I appeared on the scene. Initially and immediately it is also a glass to me and seems to be that in reality itself. In the same way, the world, even the physical world, is *primarily* a social reality to man; even the designation of this world as a "terrestrial globe" is an interpretation that has a very exact historical date. This is the reason for saying that the "world" is, first of all, a system of conventions.

As a matter of fact, interpretations are characterized by their having predated our own appearance in the world. They are not thought of as interpretations—this only occurs when they are traced to their origins, when they are seen coming into being and do not yet function as reality. Interpretations are prior to my life and are always essentially "old"; in this sense, the world is also previous to me. Strictly speaking, if there were merely "things" as such, the advent of man into the world of things would be determined by physical criteria and would imply no further complexities. But as we have seen, these "things," by virtue of their being interpretative of all nature and in view of the pressing need to shape interpretations of them, are intrinsically affected by a temporal factor. Man's appearance in the world, far from occurring at random, takes place at a specified historical level.

Let us turn now to the other term of the expression which concerns us: system of *vigencias*. The world forms the environment in which I must live; it is the scenario of my life. I am the center of my world, which functions as a totality. Hence I must consider it in its entirety, and this total consideration changes the world into a hierarchical reality. The world is, then, a closed unit, and one of its features is this very fact of its being enclosed. But in the realm of human things, one must always stop short of extremes: to state that the world is a closed unit is to say that it *tends* to be so. Such determinations refer primarily to the aims or "necessities" of man; and man does in fact *need* a closed or confined world. But there are two essential ways of opening a breach in this snug world. The first is the future: since it is not yet here, my life is not yet complete. In this sense the world is not complete and may be thought of as "open." Secondly, the world has fissures or cracks, splits or voids, which we call problems. If I cannot find an interpretation for something, a void or fissure appears in my world. There may be several reasons for an interpretation not being possible: something is new and no interpretation has yet been made of it, an old interpretation has been discredited but has yet to be replaced by another, there is a lack of cohesion or coherency among several interpretations. One of the central themes of philosophy originates in this idea of fissures: the problem of truth.[9]

Man needs to cover and fill these voids, and to embellish this world in which he must live. Inexorably, man must fashion a portion of the world, using the materials at hand in his environment. "With greater or lesser activity, originality, and energy," wrote Ortega, "man fashions his world constantly. We have already seen that the world and universe are but a scheme or interpretation which man forges to make his life secure. We may say then that the world is the instrument par excellence which man produces, and that its production is synonymous with his life and being. Man is a born maker of universes. This is why, gentlemen, we have history, why we have unending variation in human lives. If we select any date in the human past, we always find man living in a world which can be likened to a house he has built to shelter himself. This world gives him assurance in confronting certain problems which circumstance poses, but it

9. Ibid., Chapter 2.

92

leaves many problematic chasms, many unresolved and unavoidable dangers. Man's life, the drama of his life, assumes a different profile according to the perspective of his problems, according to the equation of safeguards and perils which his world represents."[10]

Man interposes projects between himself and reality, and as he goes about planning these tasks, things—hitherto mere facilities or difficulties—become possibilities. The same ground is the distance separating me from my destination and the road that leads me to it; the same wind can swell the sails of my boat or bring clouds that get in the way of my navigation. Our body, which is the greatest facility and the source of countless possibilities, becomes the greatest obstruction if it allows me to be thrown in prison or be shot. In other words, the very structure of the world is determined by the different life plans or projects that men cast over it. These projects alter the reality of things, and once they have become descriptive, they are encountered by other men who are obliged to take them into account. Such projects function, then, as objective ingredients of this new world in which men must live. A thing is in force, I repeat, when it is imposed on me and when I must take it into account regardless of my wishes. But the fact that something is in force does not mean necessarily that it is accepted. Prevailing conventions are imposed on me; my reaction to them is not. Thus it cannot be inferred that men living under the same conventions must all be alike. They must be likened in only one respect: their reactions, however different and opposing they may be, are reactions to the same reality. We see that at each historical moment there is necessarily innovation precisely because the world is different at each moment; we see also that this innovation is common to all the men of that particular moment.

10. "En torno a Galileo," *Obras completas,* V, p. 33.

It is a question of understanding human variations by means of history. Above all, a hierarchy among these variations must be established. Some changes are more general than others: some are superficial, others affect the deepest strata; some, regardless of their importance, occur by chance, others are rooted in the very structure of human life. The most important factor and the source of secondary variations, says Ortega, is ". . . the primary feeling toward life," ". . . the manner life assumes in its undifferentiated entirety." "What we shall call 'vital sensitivity' is the primary phenomenon in history and the first thing we would define in order to understand an era."[11]

But not all variations of vital sensitivity are alike. If they only affect certain individuals, they are without historical transcendence extending to multitudes. On the other hand, these variations are the work of certain outstanding individuals. Ortega insists on his doctrine of masses and select minorities as functional and dynamic elements in any society. "Human masses are receptive; they are limited to favoring or opposing men of personal and initiative life. But on the other hand, the solitary individual is an abstraction. Historical life is coexistence. An outstanding individual's life consists precisely of an all-embracing influence on the masses. It is not possible, then, to separate 'heroes' from the masses. It is a question of a duality essential to the historical process. Humanity, in all stages of its evolution, has always been a functional structure in which the most energetic men—whatever the form of that energy—have acted on the masses, giving them a certain configuration. This implies a certain basic community between superior individuals and the vulgar multitude."[12]

Here is precisely where we find that reality called generations. None of the steps we have taken so far was superfluous, but it is

11. "El tema de nuestro tiempo," *Obras completas,* III, p. 146.
12. Ibid., p. 147.

only upon reaching this point that the idea of generations is fully justified and understandable. In this context Ortega arrives at his exact and rigorous concept: "The variations of vital sensitivity that are decisive in history appear in the form of generations. A generation is not a handful of outstanding men, nor simply a mass of men; it resembles a new integration of the social body, with its select minority and its gross multitude, launched upon the orbit of existence with a pre-established vital trajectory. The generation is a dynamic compromise between mass and individual, and is the most important conception in history. It is, so to speak, the pivot responsible for the movements of historical evolution."[13]

This definition is the point of departure and it is further refined and made more precise. "A generation is a human variety"; ". . . *each generation represents a certain vital level*, from which existence is felt in a certain way. If we consider the total evolution of a people, each of its generations appears to us as a moment of its life, as a pulsation of its historical energy. And each pulsation has a peculiar and unique characteristic; it is an essential beat in the pulse, as is each note in the composition of a melody. Similarly we may imagine each generation as a species of biological missile hurled into space at a given instant, with a certain velocity and direction."[14]

The most important fact is that ". . . generations are born one of another, so that a new generation finds itself amidst the forms of existence bequeathed by those past. For each generation, then, living is a two-dimensional task; one of these consists of

13. Ibid., p. 147.
14. Ibid., p. 148. Ortega adds this note to the last sentence: "The terms 'biology,' 'biological,' are used in this book—save for some exceptions—to designate the science of life, understanding by the latter a reality in which the differences between soul and body are secondary." We shall have to take up this point again later.

receiving what the preceding generation has lived: ideas, values, institutions, etc.; the other, of allowing its own spontaneous impulses to be expressed."[15] There are "cumulative" periods during which the new generation feels itself as one with the preceding generation and stands with the older group still in power. And there are "eliminatory" and "polemic" periods, generations of combat, which sweep away the old and begin new things. There appear as separate groups among "contemporaries" (those living at the same time) those who are "coetaneous" (those of the same age): old men, young men, etc.—that is, the diverse generations coexisting at a given historical moment. And with this we again take up the theme of age.

"Strictly speaking," says Ortega, "any historical present, any so-called 'today' envelops three different times, three different 'todays' or, stated in another way, the present has a wealth of three great vital dimensions. These dimensions coexist within that 'today,' and regardless of other considerations, are intertwined with each other; but since they are different from one another, that coexistence is necessarily one of essential hostility."[16] "Contemporary men are not coetaneous: it behooves us to distinguish coetaneity from contemporaneity in history. Within a single external and chronological time, three different vital times coexist. This is what I am used to calling the essential anachronism of history. Thanks to this inner imbalance history moves, changes, advances, and flows. If all contemporary men were coetaneous, history would come to a creaky halt, and this would remain its definitive form with no possibility of any radical innovation."[17]

Specifically, what are these human ages? We may consider life

15. Ibid., pp. 148–49.
16. *En torno a Galileo,* p. 37.
17. Ibid., p. 38.

as divided into five periods of fifteen years each, making a total of seventy-five years.

1. The first fifteen years: *childhood.* There is no historical participation; what the child receives from the world hardly has a historical character. Hence the child's world changes much less from one period to another than does the adult's during the same dates.[18]

2. From fifteen to thirty: *youth.* A person is receptive to his surroundings: he sees, hears, reads, learns, and in general permits himself to be permeated by the preexisting world that he had no part in making. This is a period of learning and passivity.

3. From thirty to forty-five: *initiation.* Man now begins to act, to try to modify the inherited world, trying to impose his own innovation on it. This is the period of preparation, during which man struggles with the preceding generation and attempts to remove it from power.

4. From forty-five to sixty: *dominance.* The world man tried to begin at an earlier age now prevails. The men of this age "are in power" in every walk of life; it is the period of control. Yet at the same time these men prepare to defend this world against innovations proposed by the younger generation.

5. From sixty to seventy-five, or more in cases of great longevity: *old age.* These are men who are survivors from past periods. Hence we see immediately that a quantitative factor must be considered, for there are fewer men of this age than in the previous groups. Old men, says Ortega, are "outside of life," and this is the rôle they must play; that is, they are witnesses to a

18. In reading the splendid *Automoribundia* of Ramón Gómez de la Serna, I was struck by the relative similarity between the Madrid of his childhood around the nineties, and mine around 1920 or 1925. This resemblance is much greater than that between his adult world and the present, or between the Madrid of older people during the same periods.

previous world who carry over their experience in that world while remaining aloof from contemporary struggles. Such is the function of senates and councils of elders. But keep in mind what I said earlier about the change in the rhythm of human ages: today there are beginning to be many more men over sixty than in previous times, and furthermore many then are remaining fully active. Moreover, doctors have recently invented "geriatrics," analogous to pediatrics, offering the hope that increasingly the articulation of ages will be changed even more and that old age may be confined to the last decades of a hundred-year life.

How does this historical change occur in relation to successive generations? The sum total of young people at any given moment of time acts on the entire world. In this way, though the change brought about by any one person may be minimal, the most important fact is that—over against individual changes and regardless of their individual importance—taken together they represent a total modification and thus change the world into *another world* to a greater or lesser degree. Now that the notion of coetaneity has been brought into focus, Ortega is able to arrive at a definition of generations in the strictest sense: "The sum total of those who are coetaneous in a circle of current coexistence, is a generation. The concept of generation implies primarily only two requisites: to be the same age and to have some vital contact."[19]

But at this point a question arises: what is meant by "being the same age"? "Although it may seem incredible," writes Ortega, "again and again attempts have been made to reject *a limine* the generational method by offering the ingenuous argument that men are born every day, and therefore that only those born on the same day would be in the strictest sense the same age. Hence the generation is a chimera, an arbitrary concept representing no

19. *En torno a Galileo*, p. 38.

reality." "But it should have been realized that the concept of age is a vital, rather than a mathematical, matter. Age in the original meaning is not a date. Before men knew how to count, primitive societies appeared and still appear organized in classes based on age. Within the human life trajectory, age implies a certain mode of living. Stated in another way, an age is a life within our total life with a beginning and an ending. One begins to be a youth and one ceases to be so, just as one begins to live and stops living. Age, then, is not a date, but a 'zone of dates,' and not only those born in the same year, but also those born within a zone of dates, are the same age vitally and historically."[20]

This objection arises from two interrelated errors. The first is the insistence on individual life, and especially on genealogy, owing to an ignorance of the true "location" of generations, i.e., historical and social life. The second is traceable to biologism, the belief that human reality is fundamentally biological and that the different ages are properly ages of the organism. For this reason, the continuous nature of generations is stressed with the undeniable continuity of births as evidence. This has the effect of dissolving the generations, or when they are thought of in the usual sense, they are interpreted as mere temporal groupings succeeding and replacing each other. But "this presupposes," Ortega points out, "that man is essentially his body and his soul. All my thought runs counter to this erroneous notion. Man is primarily his life—a certain trajectory with the maximum amount of time preestablished. Age . . . is above all a portion of this trajectory and not a state of mind or body. The essential discovery we make, that in speaking of man the substantive portion is his life and all the rest adjectival, that man is a drama, a destiny and not a thing, gives us a sudden insight into this whole problem. Our several ages are the ages of our life and not

20. Ibid., pp. 40–41.

primarily of our organism. They are different stages into which our vital task is segmented. Remember that life is but that which we must do, it is something we must make for ourselves. And each age implies a peculiar portion of this task."[21]

This leads us to a most important consequence. If we focus our attention on the age of greatest historical effectiveness, we find that it is divided into two phases: men of thirty to forty-five (the period of preparation) and men of forty-five to sixty (period of control). These men live in a world of their own making, while those younger are making their world, a world not yet come into its own. Ortega observes that no two life tasks or structures are more different than these. Here are two generations seeking the same things, even to the point of fighting each other. In other words, they are contemporaneous and fully active. They are neither successive nor coetaneous: ". . . the decisive element in the idea of generations is not that they succeed each other, but rather that they overlap and touch. There are ever two generations acting at the same time, fully active as it were, regarding the same themes and concerned about the same things. But this is done with a different age index and therefore with a different meaning."[22]

Ortega distinguishes two very different types of historical change: first, when something in our world changes, and second, when the world itself changes. The latter change occurs normally and inexorably with each generation, bringing about a greater or a lesser variation—the magnitude of change is secondary—in the general world tonality. When such change is quantitatively very pronounced, and especially when instead of veering toward an adjacent system of beliefs, man is left without beliefs—and hence without a world—one may speak of a "historical crisis." A

21. Ibid., pp. 46–47.
22. Ibid., p. 49.

"decisive generation" is one that ". . . for the first time thinks the new thoughts with full clarity and with complete possession of their meaning, a generation that is neither still a precursor nor any longer bound by the past." Descartes' generation was one such.

No historical event, regardless of its gravity, can determine historical stages; the variation occasioned by a single event will always be partial. We find rather the contrary: far from determining generational succession, a given event is experienced by the generations from different temporal coefficients. That is, each generation accepts the event according to its total way of life. With this in mind we may avoid two errors that it is important to avoid.

All young people experience an event in essentially the same way because it occurs at the same stage in their life; that is, the event has the same functional meaning within their biographies. Hence it is unimportant whether one is a year older or younger than others of one's generation. Biological age is an abstract component of our life and that of generations—a necessary component but one that of itself explains nothing. Its importance is secondary, like the physical weight of our body or our size. Clearly, if man weighed only a few grams or several tons, if he were an organism five centimeters or ten meters tall, then his life would be different: physical attributes condition life. But they do not explain it or play the decisive rôle in it. For life consists of what man *does* with his weight and height, his biological age, the pull of gravity, the resistant soil under his feet, and the infinite number of other ingredients of his circumstance or world. For this reason, though we all know when we were born and that one date of birth determines whether we belong to a certain generation, our simply being aware of this date is insufficient for us to know which is our generation. For a generation is not a matter of individual life but of the objective structures of the historical world.

The second error lies in forgetting that whereas life is multiple, this multiplicity of dimensions does not alter the decisive fact that life in its totality is a unit. Thus it is not possible to formulate an adequate theory of generations limited to considerations of politics, art, or literature. Generations affect life in its totality. Certain areas of reality may be set apart, of course, but only on the condition that we remember that such areas are abstractions and not real. Generations, as men have known and forgotten a hundred times since John Stuart Mill, arise from the entire society and not from an abstract collectivity.

What, then, is a generation? It depends on the entire system of prevailing *vigencias* that lend structure to life at a certain date in history. Such a system has a certain duration and exercises its conventionalizing influence over all men who enter historical life within this time span. It is a world, therefore, that each man finds and into which he is incorporated. It is something that exceeds individual life, something that imposes itself on life and conditions it. For this reason, since we are dealing with a matter that is not biological or even biographical, determining the generation to which a man belongs requires much more than a knowledge of when he was born: we must also know the *structure* of the world at that time, which is to say: we need to know the real demarcations of generations as systems of prevailing conventions, before we can know that a particular individual is of this or that generation and not some other one. This leads to the evident consequence that each man finds himself at a certain level within his generation: at the beginning, in the middle, or at the end of it. When man appears on the scene of historical life, the system to which he is ascribed has already been prevalent for a time. Until the demarcations of generations are known, we do not know whether two men born close together but not at the same time belong to the same generation. It is necessary to know the "dividing" lines, the terminal dates of generations, for only then does the birth information acquire its historical meaning as it is viewed against the objective structure of society. Historical succession cannot be pictured as a plain on which only absolute linear distances are measured; it is, rather, a land creased by mountain ranges. In this analogy, each generation would be the area between two mountainous chains, and in order to determine whether a certain point belonged to one or the other, it would be necessary to know the relief. Two widely separated points could belong to the same generation, or two close points, on the other hand, might belong to different generations: it would depend on whether the points were on the same slope or on different sides of a divide.

This is the real nature of generations, the feature that converts them into the actual steps of historical happenings and makes of each generation what I have called the *elemental historical present*. The idea of generations, says Ortega, is "the visual organ with which historical reality can be seen in its real and vibrant authenticity," "The generation is one and the same as the structure of human life at any given moment. It is idle to try to find out what really happened at such and such a date if one does not ascertain to which generation it happened, that is, within which form of human existence it occurred. The same event happening to two different generations is a vital and hence historical reality which is completely different in each case."[23]

There is in history, then, a multiplicity of structures or, better stated, a tense, dynamic, and multiple structure. Any moment of history, no matter how fleeting, is always moving and never fixed. It always appears as a distension of three forces, of three

23. Ibid., p. 55.

generations acting at any given date; hence its reality is intrinsically mobile. We must eliminate historical Eleaticism, the tena-
cious notion that movement can be interspersed with periods of
repose. The belief that being is stationary has its final repercussion in the belief in the rigid forms of history. In our time this
notion has enjoyed a revival—in many ways quite splendid—in
the interpretation of history as a morphology. Historical forms
are not results but "resultants" in a sense analogous to that of the
physicist when he speaks of the resultant of a composition of
forces acting on a point.[24]

We must raise now the question of how long a generation
lasts, of the distance between those mountainous ranges that
comprise what I have called the "relief" of history. It is the
structure of human ages, understood as functional historical realities, that determines it. Man's fully historical participation in
events lasts, as we have seen, for thirty years. But this period is
divided into two phases that are different and even opposite in
nature: fifteen years of preparation and fifteen of acting. From
thirty to forty-five man struggles to impose a certain world
structure; from forty-five to sixty—approximately—he triumphs
and is "in power" until fifteen years later, when a new ascendant
generation imposes its innovations and displaces from authority
—in all areas of life—the convictions, usages, and ideas characteristic of the earlier period. This is why the *vigencia* of that
form of life lasts fifteen years approximately; this marks the
duration of a generation. "The system of *vigencias*," writes Or-

24. This explains the inadequacies, despite their splendid qualities and even genius, of some of the best historical books of our
time: Spengler, Huizinga, Hazard. Just imagine how much better
would have been the latter's delightful and intelligent books, *The
Crisis of European Conscience* and *European Thought in the Eighteenth Century,* had he but applied two ideas in them: that of generations and the difference between ideas and beliefs.

tega, "in which the form of human life resides, lasts for a period that almost coincides with the fifteen-year span. A generation is a zone of fifteen years during which a certain form of life was predominant. The generation would be, then, the concrete unit of authentic historical chronology; or, stated in another way, history moves and proceeds by generations. Now the true affinity between the men of a generation can be understood. Their affinity does not arise so much from themselves as from being obliged to live in a world of a certain and unique form."[25]

But even with all this we still do not know *which* generations: we know that generations exist, we know how long they endure, but we are in the dark as to their specific existence. We have not the least hint of their real succession and for this reason we continue to be unable to specify the generation to which we ourselves belong. The fact is that we are dealing here only with the analytical *theory* of generations, and this has nothing to do with their empirical existence. We shall have to pose at a later point the historical problem of that existence, and with it, the problem of the methodological meaning of the idea of generations.

Nevertheless, there remains an essential empirical item that belongs to the analytical theory, namely, the existence in all societies of a mass and a guiding minority. The latter is no abstraction such as the distinction between a political, literary, or artistic "life" or, for that matter, between all other abstract "societies" separated from the total society. As we have observed, the theory of generations cannot be applied to such abstractions, except in a sense of exemplification or didactic simplification and even then only with full and continuing awareness of their abstract quality. But the distinction between mass and guiding minority is perfectly real; it is a functional structure of the

25. *Obras completas,* VI, p. 371.

collective body. And it is functional to such a degree that one is not a member of either mass or select minority *a nativitate,* but rather on the basis of the rôle or function *fulfilled* in society. No one may sit back at ease, confident of one's status as a select-man, because hardly does one abandon the tension and effort to be such than one starts *behaving* as a mass-man. And no one is condemned to be only of the mass, for as soon as one begins to demand more of oneself and to live authentically, one rises above the mass and joins the guiding minority.

How does this distinction affect generations? Lack of clarity on this point has been a frequent source of error. Dilthey understood a generation to be "a narrow circle of individuals," that is, *qualified* individuals, and this is only a minority. When we speak of the "Generation of 1898" and shun the fact that as a generation this date merely belongs to it, we refer to a group—not even the guiding minority, but rather to eponyms (Unamuno, Baroja, Azorín, Maeztu, Valle-Inclán, Machado) who give the generation a name. In any generation, then, as a historical level, we find a mass or multitude and a guiding minority in which the essence of the generation is revealed and which lends the generation its notoriety and historical relief.

But Ortega has said that along with the great mass majority of those who insist on established ideology there is also "a small minority of minds in the vanguard, alert souls who glimpse untouched areas in the distance."[26] Are coetaneous masses and minorities of different generations? Does this not explain why that minority "lives condemned not to be fully understood," since "the actions caused by the vision of new horizons cannot be rightly interpreted by the advancing rear guard masses who still have not reached the heights from which the *terra incognita* can be observed"? This seems a highly plausible interpretation of the

26. "El tema de nuestro tiempo," *Obras completas,* III, p. 146.

situation. But once again, to forget the authentic reality and "ontological location" of generations is to fall into error.

In point of fact, there *is* a disjunction between minority and mass. However, this affects only individuals as such and does not preclude a perfect synchronization in collective matters. This is so even to the point that the outstanding man, as an individual, may reject and struggle against certain things and yet, as a member of society and a man of his time, accept those same things as the prevailing modes. A great portion of the individual is immersed in the social, imbued with it, molded of the same substance. "Tell me who your friends are and I will tell you who you are," goes the Spanish saying. Each of us moves with the men of our generation, submerged in the great anonymous multitude, and save for the final individual nucleus of our life, to ask ourselves to which generation we belong is, in large measure, to ask *who* we are.

4

Vicissitudes of
the Generations Theme
in Our Century

ORTEGA'S THEORY OF GENERATIONS HAS ENABLED US TO understand not only what they are but also what might be called their "ontological location"—social and historical life—and the mechanism of their historical functioning. Before considering the problems of their concrete existence and their methodological meaning, we should give brief attention to what others in this century have contributed to generational thinking, especially in Germany. Ortega's theory will serve as a backdrop against which the other views will stand out in bolder relief, and it will be for us an example of what a theory is—a standard of comparison. The bibliography on the theme is quite rich, quantitatively at least, but I am going to touch only on the highpoints that constitute a new contribution or a representative way of focusing on the question.[1] More often than I should like, I shall have to stress certain deficiencies and errors, for it cannot be said that the theme of generations has received the most fortunate of treatment in recent years. The most concentrated interest has coin-

1. The bibliography at the end of this book lists several works that need not be treated in detail in this study.

cided with the prevalence of certain intellectual conventions involving considerable risks. The reason I take the time to point out and underscore some of these deficiencies is the possibilities they offer for revealing certain facets of contemporary intellectual life. The fact that serious deficiencies are occasionally found in the work of highly esteemed and competent authors is the point of greatest interest, perhaps, for it draws our attention to certain negative aspects of the society of our time that transcend individuals and even occasionally eclipse their excellent personal qualities. We shall find welcome exceptions, both in Spain and elsewhere, but more often we shall encounter defective intellectual attitudes, the root of which, if we look closely, is moral and buried in the collective environment. It is high time to remove any doubt that what is called "talent" is, for the most part, a moral condition. And if we compare these doctrines about generations to Ortega's theory, we shall see that everyone has given the theme a rather narrow treatment, and that none of those acquainted with Ortega's theory—all of the Spaniards and almost all of the Germans—has understood it precisely and adequately.

François Mentré

François Mentré, who was very much influenced by Cournot (to whom he has dedicated some excellent works), published a book in 1920 entitled *Les générations sociales* [Social Generations].[2] It received much less attention than it deserved. The first

2. I owe my knowledge of Mentré's book to Ortega. This work has been useful to me, putting me on the track of various ideas. It is a curious thing that in spite of the evident interest the book would have for those concerned, it seems not to be known to those who have treated the generation theme. I have only found a brief mention of the work in Mannheim, and it is probable that he was

part of the book—a history of the problem of generations and of previous theories down to the time of Lorenz—is by far the best treatment of the theme, especially for that period, among extant works. Although there are a few important omissions and the significance of some theories is not correctly interpreted, the historical portion of the work is by and large a very sound and accurate presentation, with abundant first-hand documentation. The second part, dedicated to "facts and hypotheses," contains Mentré's personal opinions on the topic. It is to this part that I shall mainly refer. The third part is an attempt to apply the theory, with emphasis on French generations from 1515 to 1914.

Mentré does not try to state a new theory of human generations, but rather to rid the concept of the almost mystical elements with which Dromel, Ferrari, and Lorenz had burdened it. He wishes to uncover and retain the abiding elements of the concept and to prove its validity.[3] His reflections on the theme, as he says, began prior to the search for historical antecedents, in which he tried to find stimuli, acquired results, and orientation toward new points of view.[4] This modesty and moderation of purpose is usually accompanied by considerable contributions in practice. Strictly speaking, Mentré goes as far as the intellectual instruments he manipulates will allow him, and his constant penetration and good sense prove beyond doubt the inescapable need for an adequate theory—one that is philosophical in nature —of historical and social reality, in order to be able to formulate a precise theory of generations. For lack of such a theory, Mentré appears uncertain far more often than not, and his assertions,

---

largely unfamiliar with Mentré's work, since he does not include in his study other books cited by Mentré in his (Henri Peyre also cites him in his *Les générations littéraires* [1948]).

3. *Les générations sociales,* p. 464.
4. Ibid., pp. 7–8.

though often true, seem unsure and contradictory from page to page. What we find, then, are many accurate observations obedient to a reality whose true nature eludes him.

What is a generation? Mentré begins by distinguishing between family or genealogical and social generations. A social generation is "a group of men belonging to different families. Its unity results from a particular mentality and its duration spans a specific period."[5] This exceedingly vague and provisional definition is the one he must clarify and make scientific. All contemporaries are included in a social generation and yet, Mentré notes, children are not of the same group as parents. This leads him to the problem of the duration of generations and of distinguishing between them. Mentré reviews the existing solutions, from the identification of the social generation with the family generation—some thirty years—and concludes that no rational solution to the problem is possible: any specific duration that may be proposed encounters theoretically insurmountable obstacles.[6] In the end he decides that a generation's duration is determined by the active and mature years of its leaders and principal followers.[7] Thus, but for different reasons than the genealogists, he falls back on the approximate figure of thirty years. He fails to see, however, that since thirty years is the duration not of a man's historical action but of the predominance of a certain world form, the real and effective duration of a generation is reduced to half that figure. A generation is, then, in summary: "A state of collective mind embodied in a human

5. Ibid., p. 13.
6. "Pure reason is powerless to stop debate. In fact, whatever the length of time assigned to the social generation, one finds obstacles to the choice that are *theoretically insurmountable*" (Ibid., p. 30).
7. Ibid., p. 44.

group that endures for a certain time, analogous to the duration of a family generation."[8] At times Mentré seems close to sensing what generations really are: "All the men of a generation feel bound together by a common point of departure, by their beliefs and desires. The power of circumstances has imposed on them a collective program which they carry out more or less through their willing or casual association."[9] But how deeply is this idea impressed on the author's mind? He clarifies it for us when he declares: "The basis for any theory of generation can only be psychological; what differentiates one generation from those preceding or following is its psychology, that is, the sum of its beliefs and its desires."[10] What we have, then, is not social and historical life, not a prevailing *world* structure, but a psychological reality that leads in short to individual life where the collective is meaningful only in approximate and comparative terms. He goes on to insist on the same ideas with formulas that reveal even more explicitly both his insight and his deficiencies: "A generation is characterized neither by its knowledge nor by its material capability. . . . Knowledge and technology do not define man. A generation can only be defined in terms of beliefs, and desires, in psychological and moral terms."[11] "Hence a generation is *a way of experiencing and understanding life* that is contrary to, or at least different from, previous modes."[12]

This discrepancy between the truth of his observations and the faults of his theoretical suppositions is evident throughout the book. A generation is "a particular shade of sensitivity," "an attitude toward life."[13] "It is not events that mark generations,

8. Ibid., p. 40.
9. Ibid., pp. 47–48.
10. Ibid., p. 172.
11. Ibid., p. 298.
12. Ibid., p. 304.
13. Ibid., pp. 342–43.

but generations that mark events."[14] Yet on the other hand it seems to him beyond doubt that "a generation is a biological reality," and that the social and the psychological are based on, and conditioned by the biological.[15] The notion of the generation appears as a *working hypothesis*[16] that may be true or false but is useful and productive in either case because it brings order and clarity to facts. Mentré is methodically confident, so much so that for him "general history, history as lived by the masses of men, is impossible without the idea of generations."[17]

We shall see just how impossible a theory of generations was before philosophy had taken certain decisive steps, which came about only in Ortega's work. If it had been possible to formulate such a theory with other, less refined philosophical instruments, and without a precise idea of the nature of human, individual, and collective life, then Mentré, who was quite well versed in the antecedents of the theme and was an astute observer of facts, surely would have done so. He sees the phenomenon of generations much better than later and more ambitious theoreticians. This explains his ability to accumulate accurate and suggestive observations on the function and historical rôle of generations. Even so, their essence and authentic reality elude him, as does a true grasp of that dimension of reality in which generations occur.

Wilhelm Pinder

The German bibliography on the generations theme, after Lorenz (1891), is concentrated in the few years between 1926 and 1933. Before these dates we find only the application of previous doctrines that are irrelevant from a theoretical point of

14. Ibid., p. 451.
15. Ibid., p. 462.
16. Ibid., p. 463.
17. Ibid., p. 298.

view; Kummer, H. V. Muller, W. Vogel, K. Joël, *et al.*[18] The earliest and also the most interesting and valuable contribution to this almost simultaneous production is the work of Wilhelm Pinder.

Pinder treats the problem of generations in his contribution to a *Festschrift* honoring Volkelt: *Kunstgeschichte nach Generationen. Zwischen Philosophie und Kunst. Johann Volkelt zum 100. Lehrsemester Dargebracht* [The History of Art According to Generations. Between Philosophy and Art. Presented to Johann Volkelt on his Hundredth Semester of Teaching] (Leipzig, 1926), and in a book, published in Berlin later in that same year, in which we find a more mature expression of his ideas: *Das Problem der Generation in der Kunstgeschichte Europas* [The Problem of Generation in the History of European Art]. A second edition of the work appeared in 1928 with a new and important prologue.[19]

Pinder begins by applying the idea of generations to a particular theme, and moves on to general theoretical considerations only as the problems posed by this application oblige him to do so. However, these considerations remain closely tied to the original theme of art. Naturally, I shall refer here only to the theory, leaving aside Pinder's crudite, suggestive, but disputable applications of the theory to art history. Pinder's doctrine is so conditioned by art history that what really interests him is the idea—penetrating and fertile to be sure, but removed from the central question—that the different arts, in a figurative and allegorical sense, can be interpreted as "generations."[20] With this in mind, he writes: "My basic thought deals even more with the

18. Cf. the bibliographical references at the end of the book.

19. My references are to the Spanish edition of Wilhelm Pinder's *El problema de las generaciones en la historia del arte de Europa*, Trans. D. J. Vogelmann (Buenos Aires, 1946).

20. Ibid., pp. 173–92.

relation, similar to that of generations, among the arts themselves, than with the actual generational relationship between artists themselves."[21]

Pinder calls his book "an attempt at a biology of the sciences of the mind,"[22] and adds: "this book is a conscious attempt to transpose the antithesis between natural sciences and those of the mind. The destiny of my generation may be to insist on the unity of nature and mind (in any case this generation has Goethe on its side), and to dedicate itself to physiognomic interpretations and character studies of men, peoples, cultures, generations, and terrestrial periods. Klages, Spengler, Dacqué, Nadler—these are some of the 'suspicious' names we may consider in this regard." Furthermore, Pinder finds psychological explanations insufficient, and his attitude is one of "skepticism regarding one's ever reaching a complete explanation of life."[23] Hence his insistence on birth as a decisive factor in generations, and his appeal to the Aristotelian concept of "entelechy" as a way of understanding them. The biologist Hans Driesch had advocated the same concept, but with a different meaning.

Pinder's guiding idea is "the contemporaneity of that which is not coetaneous," which is to say the distinction between contemporaneity (*Gleichzeitigkeit*) and coetaneity (*Gleichaltrigkeit*).[24]

21. Ibid., p. 15.
22. Ibid., p. 19.
23. Ibid., p. 27.
24. Ibid., pp. 45 ff. In the Prologue to the second edition, Pinder refers to Ortega's *El tema de nuestro tiempo* [The Modern Theme], published in German in 1928: "I find the finest corroboration of my conviction, however, in my own case, in the Spanish philosopher José Ortega" (p. 39). He cites long paragraphs from Ortega's works, although he also omits some very essential ones and does not see that the idea of coetaneity is already contained in

At any given moment in time men of all ages are alive, and a theory of generations must take this fundamental fact into consideration. Unlike Eduard Wechssler, for example, who interprets Stefan George in terms of the *George-Kreis,* the "circle" of young men who surrounded him, Pinder rightly turns to George's generation, to his coevals who were, perhaps, unknown. Likewise—and unlike Alfred Lorenz—he will not include Mozart (born in 1756) and Beethoven (born in 1770) in the same generation: "On the contrary," he writes, "I would assign two such influential masters, whose birthdays are separated by half a human lifetime, to two different historical generations, even were they by some strange miracle sons of the same father and therefore in the same generation from the naturalistic point of view."[25] With this Pinder surpasses both the idea of a common psychology and of inter-individual life and the genealogical interpretation of generations.

"These simple 'presents,' " Pinder goes on to say, "have no absolute existence, since in reality every historical moment is being lived by men of varying stages of historical duration, [men] for each of whom this moment means something different, *even a different age!*"[26] If we take a precise date, a year, and consider it as a temporal point, we note that in the strictest sense it is not a point but a line, "a *depth sounding* that we drop vertically through life developments, through connections of the history of forms, connections that reveal varying beginning points and differing prospects of endurance. *Any historical 'tem-*

---

the work. This idea also appears as an epigraph in an Ortegan work of 1924.

25. Ibid., p. 40. Nevertheless, Pinder exaggerates the temporal distance separating the two musicians. It would take no miracle for them to be sons of the same father.

26. Ibid., p. 50.

poral point' is at the very least a sounding. Hence it is not a point but a line."[27] And he concludes by saying: "All this translated into human terms would be: each person lives with his coevals and with persons of different ages within a plenitude of simultaneous possibilities. For each person the same time period is at once a different age, that is, different *as far as he is concerned.* Only his coevals share his view of the period. Each point of time means something different to each person, not only because obviously it is experienced by each person individually, but also because the same year, as a 'point of real time' underlying all individual coloration, constitutes for a man of fifty a temporal point within his life that is completely different from that of a twenty-year-old man. And so we have a series of infinite variants."[28]

This is Pinder's principal idea, his true contribution—quite apart from its application to art—to generations theory. But when he begins to try to clarify what generations consist of, the clarity vanishes. He begins with what he calls "the fact of regular grouping of decisive births, in obedience to a law: the decisive births in nature."[29] "Nature," he adds, "permits rhythmic pauses between a succession of births of leading minds."[30] Artists are bound to their time; their birth determines the development of their being and predetermines their problems. This does not isolate them in time, however, but instead groups them into generations. Overlying the rhythm of epochs, there is a rhythm of generations.[31]

But what is the nature of these generations? Pinder falters on

27. Ibid., p. 57.
28. Ibid., pp. 58–59.
29. Ibid., p. 63.
30. Ibid., p. 63.
31. Ibid., p. 65.

the traditional objection: the continuity of births. He realizes that "a generation is an abstraction, but an abstraction that retains an extraordinary proximity to life. . . . In the physiological sense, a generation is of course born every minute. . . . Nevertheless, within the limits of practically possible work, there is no doubt that one can see an extreme power of contraction, which is a characteristic of certain periods, regarding these key births. There is only one way to establish the validity of such periods: birth statistics."[32] "Thus we give the name generation to a group of persons who are more or less coetaneous. We shall see that this is possible if we base it on the *intervals* appearing between the strata formed by birth rhythms."[33] This means that Pinder hopes to be able to get around the continuous-births argument by presupposing a discontinuity of *illustrious* births; the very heart of his interpretation rests on this improbable hypothesis, and it is for precisely this reason that he insists on it. But he is then obliged to set about finding these concentrations of illustrious men, these "multiple births" of nature, throughout the history of art. He must, therefore, define concrete and real generations by these concentrations of great figures, and this leads him to establish the variability of the generational intervals: "There are periods of very short intervals during which a dominant vital torrent continues to create, at extraordinarily rapid intervals, decisive clusters of births."[34] This river of life can at times "speed up the rhythm of these concentrations," or it can engender important isolated individuals who function as "transitional masters."[35]

Pinder observes a certain regularity in the length of the inter-

32. Ibid., pp. 70–72.
33. Ibid., p. 72.
34. Ibid., p. 99.
35. Ibid., pp. 156–57.

vals: "In a strange way (or perhaps a very natural one?) what we call an age, a human generation, plays a mysterious role, either as a whole or half measure. . . . But of course these units can be shorter at times: intervals of twenty and ten years, rather than thirty and fifteen."[36] Pinder summarizes by saying: *"Groupings of decisive births* exist. Hence, the *intervals* between them also exist. We have noted the tendency of nature to use the human generation (twenty-five to thirty years) as a measuring unit (taken as a whole or half unit) for these intervals. We also saw a tendency in some periods for these intervals to be shortened and for the total birthrate to increase."[37]

Pinder obviously does not know, strictly speaking, what a generation is, nor where it is to placed. His only important discovery, and I stress "important" more than "discovery," is the distinction between contemporaneity and coetaneity. His tendency is to find everything of importance in individuals and statistical groupings. In order to determine the intervals he has to turn to the uncertain and unprovable concentration of leading figures. Therefore, his idea has no general historical meaning; a generation, as he understands it, is far from being a historical category. He offers no ideas on collective life, *vigencia,* and zone dates, and as we have seen, these are basic to understanding the nature of generations. In order to explain groupings, he has to resort to vague natural metaphors ("decisive births," etc.), to that which in itself is inexplicable. As for the frequent regularity of intervals, he hesitates between seeing it as a mysterious process (appealing to vague designations or tendencies of nature) or as something quite natural (falling back on biological genealogy). Pinder's book contains a wealth of interesting and at times

36. Ibid., pp. 157–58.
37. Ibid., pp. 248–49.

profound ideas, as well as many annotated data. Even so, it does not reach the level of coherent and consistent theory of historical generations.

Julius Petersen

Julius Petersen, a literary historian, is, along with Pinder, the most widely known German writer on the generations theme. He first considers the theme in chapter 6 of his book *Die Wesensbestimmung der deutschen Romantik* [The Essence of German Romanticism] (1926). He treats it in greater depth and detail in a long study, *Die Literarischen Generationen* [Literary Generations], published in a collected volume, *Philosophie der Literaturwissenschaft* [The Philosophy of Literary Science] edited by Ermatinger (1930).[38] Finally, he summarizes his ideas in the first volume of *Die Wissenschaft von der Dichtung* [The Science of Poetry] (1939). For our purposes the second of these texts is the most important.

Petersen finds that many disciplines—among them literary history—use the concept of generations but do so in diverse and uncertain ways, while the basic notion has yet to be firmly established. "The word 'generation,'" he writes, "holds the key to the undeniable facts of change and development, progress and regression; the question is whether such a key can be manipulated like a *passepartout* to all roads or like a jimmy to break through doors, or whether it is a secret key which, like a work of very subtle art, can only be used by experts."[39] "The current use of the word," he adds, "has become so ambiguous through its

38. I quote from the Spanish translation by Fondo de Cultura Económica, which, incidentally, shows less polish and perfection than usual: Julius Petersen, *Las generaciones literarias,* included in *Filosofía de la ciencia literaria* (Mexico, 1946), pp. 137–39.
39. Ibid., pp. 138–39.

120

many definitions that it becomes necessary to examine and determine the range of its meaning by the use of some examples."[40]

He begins with the empirical material of the data he intends to place in order. While he has no underlying theory, this does not mean that he approaches his data directly and without any recourse to theory; indeed, something resembling a swarm of theories from various sources seems to be buzzing in his head. Petersen attempts to write a history of the topic, and it turns out to be a very incomplete, confused, and confusing effort indeed. His seeming *Gründlichkeit*, his thoroughness, has led many to put trust in his presumed exactness and documentation; they imagine that if they know what Petersen knows they have sufficient information. However, aside from the fact that his presentation is irregular and lacking in conceptual precision, Petersen knowingly omits all mention of Comte, Mill, Soulavie, Benloew, Ferrari, Cournot, Mentré, to say nothing of Littré and Durkheim, as well as other names appearing in the present study, which attempts to shun mere erudition and to omit unnecessary items.

Having posed the question of what a generation is, Petersen begins by dismissing the notion that a generation means the collectivity of all those of the same age. The reason for this is that he finds many persons in opposition to prevailing tendencies.[41] He also rejects the application of a chronological idea of generation to different countries: "As a temporal concept with a certain number of years, such as from 1890 to 1900, it is impossible to identify a generation with the same features in all countries with a Christian calendar. Rather, what we discover is an inner time which, like the flowering and fruiting cycle of a plant, changes from climate to climate, as different in the various

40. Ibid., p. 139.
41. Ibid., p. 143.

countries as are the meridians or the rising and setting of the sun."[42] "The problem lies in the question of whether the new will of the descendants is found to be already implied by the date of birth and thereby must needs lead to future changes, or whether this will arises from the impression left by homogeneous *vigencias* with which they are in sympathy."[43] Petersen refers to Ortega,[44] whom he knows through the German version of *The Modern Theme*. Ortega's concept of generations, says Petersen, includes the two items of similar age and direction. But he questions "whether a common direction springs from the fact of similar age or whether those of more or less the same age grow up within a pre-existing current and, because of their common age, are absorbed into this current at the same time. In a word, he concludes, "we have the question of whether the unit 'generation' is born or made."[45] But it is clear that this dilemma is meaningless, for a generation is neither born nor made. The men who make up a generation find themselves living within the same system of *vigencias* that go to make up their social world. This world conditions their lives in the sense that regardless of what they do, they do it in view of that world, as a response to a common and concrete situation. But the system does not fix what it is that they may do, and for this reason the widest range and variety of postures may be assumed by individuals, all in response to a common situation. This shared world or situation lends such men a very precise similarity: a certain "historical level" at which they live. Later we shall see the origin of this ambiguity in the stating of the problem. Obviously Petersen is heeding individual characteristics and conduct and thus has difficulty in supposing

42. Ibid., pp. 144–45.
43. Ibid., p. 145.
44. Ibid., pp. 146, 147.
45. Ibid., p. 146.

122

discrepant men to be of the same generation. "In most cases," he writes, "the fact that men come from different districts and circles has kept generational tendencies toward unity from being imposed. But there is also another factor, and this is the diversity of individual 'temperament,' which is independent of time, race, and place."[46]

Petersen tries to "combine the idea of generation with the theory of types."[47] Among those born within the same period, there are various types of dispositions or temperaments (*Anlage*); among these types there is the one that gathers the young generation under a new order, as it were. This is the "directive type of the generation" who attracts others of a different disposition and who collectively make up what Petersen calls the "directed type." The incorporation of the latter type strengthens the first and isolates a third. This group, antagonistic and without influence, is the "suppressed type." One of this type may choose to travel abandoned paths as his nature would have him do; he may subordinate himself to the dominant tendency and renounce his own peculiarity, or he may simply withdraw and await the future.

In connection with this idea—one that would be more fertile if the fact toward which it aims were rightly situated—is the theme on which Petersen places more emphasis and which has had the greatest impact: the formative factors of a generation. I shall not go into detail on all Petersen says regarding these factors. Much of what he offers is inconsistent. For our purposes we need mention only his listing of the factors: (a) heredity, (b) date of birth, (c) educational factors, (d) personal community, (e) experiences of the generation, (f) the speech of the generation, and (g) the inflexibility of the older generation.[48]

46. Ibid., p. 158.
47. Ibid., pp. 159–60.
48. Ibid., pp. 164–88.

In considering this series of factors which, according to Petersen, make up a generation, a question immediately arises: to what reality do they refer? What area of reality do they affect? Of course all of them do not point to the same reality. Some, such as heredity, are biological in emphasis; others, such as one's personal community or life experiences, deal with the sphere of individual life; and still others, such as the "guide" or "speech" of a generation (in the sense that Petersen uses these terms), correspond to abstract groups set apart from the rest of society by a common occupation. In sum, only a few belong to collective life. Petersen's work, therefore, reveals a basic confusion concerning the type of reality to be found in a generation, and a resulting inability to answer the decisive question of what a generation is.

From this essential uncertainty Petersen falls into a succession of vague notions as he tries to draw conclusions from his suppositions. He writes: "From the process noted in the formation of a generation, it follows that what is called a generation cannot be ascribed a regular span of time, which would depend on the mean duration of action of its individual members, nor can it acquire this temporal regularity by reference to birth. Rather it is to be understood as a unity of being arising from a common destiny, and this in turn implies a uniformity of experiences and aims."[49] Only in passing does Petersen ask "whether it is legitimate to limit these observations to literary generations, and whether the literary generation might not be better understood as coinciding to such a degree with political, social, and economic generations that the problem becomes one of sociology and cultural history."[50] But this suspicion, tossed in almost as an afterthought at the end of the work, is quite idle: John Stuart Mill

49. Ibid., p. 188.
50. Ibid., p. 189.

had already anticipated the question and answered it rather thoroughly in 1843! Petersen concludes that the temporal distance between generations is incalculable; the intervals between them vary and modern life has accelerated its pace. The upshot is that his concept loses all exactitude.

It is obvious that Petersen is not the master of the material with which he is dealing. He lacks a clear-cut theory, or even the rudiments of a theory such as that of Pinder. He isolates himself within intra-literary questions without ever grasping the real problem. His concentration on the unreal concept of a "literary generation" nullifies his efforts. And his late appeal to a higher reality is quite unproductive. He passes over the real questions without even perceiving them; his distinction between "directors," "the directed," and "the suppressed," which of itself is an astute observation, might have possibilities were it not interpreted as a function of the so-called "types of disposition." Likewise, his notions would have been more meaningful had he grasped the functional difference between masses and minorities, and between collective *vigencias* and individual opinions and desires. Unfortunately, Petersen chose the wrong road, and all those who have followed him along it have been led away from an understanding of generations.

Karl Mannheim

The other German studies on the generation with which I am acquainted are of lesser interest and scope. Nevertheless, several of them deserve some brief mention. One of the most serious and weighty, more critical than theoretical in content, is an essay that the great sociologist Karl Mannheim published in 1928.[51] Mann-

51. Karl Mannheim, "Das Problem der Generationen" in *Kölner Vierteljahrshefte für Soziologie,* 7. Jahrg., Hefte 2–3 (1928).

heim distinguishes two principal ways of presenting the problem: a positivistic approach based on the biological law of the duration of life divided into different ages (this is the approach that seeks in the idea of generations, a unit of measurement and the echelons of progress), and a historical–romantic view that veers more toward an idea of inner time and the historical content of the generation. The temporal magnitude or length of generations appears irregular and indeterminate, varying with historical forces. Generations resemble waves of variable size in direct relation to the intensity of the acting forces.[52]

As for Mannheim's own contribution, however, he points out three different aspects within the general sociological phenomenon. The most prominent of these is what he calls *Generationslagerung,* the "setting" or immediate locale of the generation, which holds only potential possibilities. The second aspect is *Generationszusammenhang,* generation connection or association, which adds a binding force to what hitherto is mere existence within some given socio-historical unit. Finally, he distinguishes *Generationseinheit,* or generation unit, which corresponds to a group bound by personal relationships within the connection already mentioned. Mannheim clarifies the distinction with an example: Prussian youth of 1800 were not in the same generation setting or *Generationslagerung* as Chinese youth of the same period, because they did not belong to the same common stream of history. Prussian peasants in turn, residing in remote places and removed from the social and spiritual commotions of youth in the cities, do not belong to the same *Generationszusammenhang* or generation connection as the lat-

52. Remember that in the structure of historical occurrence, one must distinguish the generations and "historical periods," the length of which is elsewhere determined. Cf. my *Introducción a la Filosofía,* Chapter 10, p. 81; and *La estructura social.*

ter, although they could perhaps be included in the same *Generationslagerung* or generational setting. The Romantic conservative youth of 1800 and their rationalistic liberal counterparts both belonged to the same *Generationszusammenhang*, but they constituted two *Generationseinheiten* or generation units. "The same youth," concludes Mannheim, "who are oriented in a common history and current problems, live in a 'generation association,' and those groups who, within the same generation connection, elaborate these experiences in different ways, constitute diverse 'generation units' within the framework of the same generation connection."[53]

Mannheim concludes his work with several observations on the interest and risks in the idea of generations. He writes that "the importance of the theories of generations consisted in the fact that they accentuated more and more a theoretical interest in the factor of human historical happening. Undoubtedly this was important, but we may say in summary that it was a one-sided view that came from trying to explain by this one factor alone the total dynamics of historical occurrence. Such a one-sided vision is always inherent in the happiness of he who discovers it and hence is forgivable."[54] But we must not forget that, in the first place, there is much more in the idea of generations as a historical category than is conceived in the theories considered by Mannheim. Secondly, indeed it is idle to try to explain history

53. In the German: "Dieselbe Jugend, die an derselben historichaktuellen Problematik orientiert ist, lebt einem 'Generationszusammenhang,' diejenigen Gruppen, die innerhalb desselben Generationszusammenhanges in jeweils verschiedener Weise diese Erlebnisse verarbeiten, bilden jeweils verschiedene 'Generationseinheiten' im Rahmen desselben Generationszusammenhanges" (*Das Problem der Generationen*, p. 311).

54. Ibid., p. 321.

solely by means of generations. In fact, once we have the subjects of historical actions and the structure of the basic present time, we still have not explained the real content of history itself.

Eduard Wechssler

The Romance scholar Eduard Wechssler set forth the generations theme from another point of view, one that in reality harks back to much earlier views. Wechssler's ideas begin with the application of Dilthey's to literary history. Wechssler expressed his ideas most fully in two articles published in 1927 and 1929: *Die Generation als Jugendgemeinschaft* [The Generation as an Inner Relation of Youth],[55] and *Das Problem der Generationen in der Geistesgeschichte* [The Problem of Generation in the History of Ideas].[56] Earlier, in an article published in 1923, *Die Auseinandersetzung des deutschen Geistes mit der französischen Aufklärung*[57] [The Perspective of the German Mind on the French Enlightenment], he had offered several observations on the topic. Specifically, he grouped the most important names of the French Enlightenment in "age communities."

Wechssler's central idea is that of "youthful community." The date of birth is not decisive. What is really important is the moment of the community's appearance in history (*kairós*). Wechssler definitely stresses the second in the series of dates that Ferrari considered important in a biography: the date of birth, "rise," and death of the individual. This "youthful community" or relationship is based on a similarity of vital temperament, of spiritual attitude, and of problems. Yet if this is so, then such a

55. In the homage to Breysig, *Geist und Gesellschaft*, I, pp. 66–102.
56. *Davoser Revue*, 4, 8.
57. Eduard Wechssler, *Deutsche Vierteljahrschift für Literaturwissenschaft und Geistesgeschichte*, I, 615.

"community" of values refers to interindividual relationships and is not properly social or collective in nature. Likewise, the appearance of a generation depends on the exhaustion of the preceding one, and points to a conscious, deliberate historical renovation devoid of regularity. Generations come and go at varying and completely unforeseeable intervals.

Engelbert Drerup

Worthy of mention, but of little else, is a book by the classical philologist Engelbert Drerup, *Das Generationsproblem in der griechischen und griechish-römischen Kultur* [The Problem of Generation in Greek and Graeco-Roman Culture] (Paderborn, 1933). Drerup's aim is to apply the idea of generations to the ancient world, and the better part of his book is devoted to this task. Only the introduction (pp. 9–25) contains any theoretical indications, and these are very brief. At the outset he accepts the definition of generation offered by Ortega in *The Modern Theme*. He attempts to place the question in perspective by means of some very sketchy historical notes referring to Greek precedents: Herodotus, Hecataeus, Hellanicus, and Ephorus. Drerup has no theory of his own, and seems to be not especially perceptive in his understanding the theories of others. This becomes quite apparent when, after quoting Ortega's second definition of generation as a "human variety," he adds: "these generational differences in a population must be understood in the light of modern racial biology,"[58] and goes on to refer to the ideas of Scheidt the biologist!

In short, Drerup falls back on the outworn notion that three generations make up a period approximating a century. He does,

58. In the German: "Diese Generationsunterschiede einer Bevölkerung aber sollen im Sinne der modernen Rassenbiologie verstanden werden" (*Das Generationsproblem*, pp. 14–15).

however, admit slight yearly variations in this scheme. Elsewhere, when attempting to apply his concept to the Graeco-Roman world, he goes so far as to admit the possibility of discord between different abstract generations (political, artistic, literary, et al.)

So far as I know at this writing, the foregoing are the principal contributions of twentieth-century German thought to the generations theme. They lead us to conclude that no one in Germany has yet come up with a theory of generations deserving of the name. Actually, little progress has been made in that country since Dilthey and Lorenz, and there have even been instances of regression. True, the notion of generation has been extended—save for an occasional lapse—from Dilthey's "narrow circle of individuals" to the whole society, and Lorenz's notions of genealogy have almost been eliminated. But there is little else. The only important discovery—its importance depends on the degree to which it can be considered a discovery—is the precise differentiation of contemporaneity and coetaneity.

Why was a true theory of generation not forthcoming in Germany? As paradoxical as it may appear, in speaking of a country with so illustrious a tradition, the reason is a lack of philosophical bases! Only in recent years, in the work of the towering philosopher Martin Heidegger, has a metaphysical interpretation of human life been conceived that surpasses Dilthey's thought. And not even in Heidegger, at least not in a current sense, do we find the elements necessary for a theory of collective life. When he encounters the generation theme in connection with the destiny and unfolding of "existence," Heidegger prefers to cite Dilthey rather than elaborate a concept of his own.[59] Sociologists, for their part, have failed to see the

59. "The inevitable link of the destiny of one's existence with and to his generation reveals the full and real unfolding of existence" (*Sein und Zeit* [1927]), pp. 384–85.

distinction between the truly social and the merely interindividual. Notwithstanding the fact that a German, Dilthey, coined the expression, what has been lacking in Germany, in the final analysis, is *historical reason*.

The absence of a generations theory was not, therefore, due to chance. But more serious even than this is the petulant and irresponsible manner in which problems have been approached by writers lacking the necessary resources to treat them. Such has not been the nature of Germans in better periods of their history, and it is for this reason that I have spent more time expounding on these doctrines than their intrinsic merits would appear to justify. In sum, then, Ortega's theory of generations is the only one up to now, and this state of affairs came about not by chance but by absolute historical necessity.

Two Objections on Principle: Croce and Huizinga

We must take note of two objections that touch on the very possibility of a doctrine of generations, not only because they are offered by two of the more important of contemporary thinkers on matters of historical theory, but also because they reveal the vagueness of the usual theories and how difficult it is, even for men of the astuteness of Croce and Huizinga, to gain an adequate perspective.

In his *Teoria e storia della storiografia* [Theory and History of Historiography], Croce criticizes the attempts of Ferrari and Lorenz to develop a system of periodicity based on generations, and extends his criticism beyond these specific examples to cover all similar theories. Croce states that all doctrines that show the history of peoples as something arising from the steps of individual or psychological evolution, or from the categories of the spirit, or from anything else, reveal the supposed periodicity to be external and natural. Such theories are naturalistic, mythological, fantastic, of no value, and hence undeserving of a detailed study.[60] But perhaps if Croce had abandoned this *a priori* judgment and considered deeply the possibilities of a theory of generations, he might have discovered that such a theory means precisely taking a point of view that is social and intrinsically historical. The theory of generations allows us to see history from within itself, situated in its own reality. Rightly understood, it entails nothing more or less than transcending naturalism in the interpretation of historical reality.

Huizinga, although assuredly one of this century's best historical thinkers, has merely skimmed over the peculiarity of generations. He has considered the matter, indeed, only long enough to offer a completely misguided objection to the theory. In his *Problemas de historia de la cultura* [Problems in the History of Culture] (1929), he recalls some antecedents of the generations theory—Cournot, Ferrari, Lorenz—and refers to more recent studies by W. Vogel, K. Joël, and Pinder. He states: "It seems to me that the new forms in which the generations theory is expressed will *never* overcome a *fundamental logical fallacy that will render them all unacceptable.* If we take a series of three generations, the first will always be second and third with respect to the two that precede it. But this alone is not the problem. One may establish a trinity of generations from 1700 to 1733, from 1734 to 1769, and from 1770 to 1800, thinking that by doing so

60. "All the doctrines that represent the history of peoples as something arising from individual or psychological development, or from the categories of the spirit or mind, or from anything else, can be traced to the same error: that of assuming periodization to be something natural and external. These are all naturalistic and mythological notions. And this thus removes any need to examine the particulars and details of these doctrines. For in this respect, if their content is visibly fantastic, their value is accordingly null" (Benedetto Croce, *Teoria e storia della storiografia,* 2nd ed. [Bari, 1920], pp. 101–2).

he is determining a series of historical phenomena that make up the eighteenth century in the following order: rise, maturity, and decadence; or action, reaction, and elaboration. But there is also a chain of generations fixed by the years 1701 to 1734, 1735 to 1770, and 1771 to 1801; these exist simultaneously with those previously listed; they show the same variation as to their initial year and practically follow the same day to day change. *From a biological viewpoint,* all these series have absolutely the same validity. . . . It is impossible to utilize the generation as such as a phase in the development of a particular historical phenomenon; for the generation, *biologically* speaking, is and always will be a completely arbitrary period of time."[61]

Huizinga's double objection is applicable only to generation theories that are afflicted with a double error: first, the establishment of groups of three generations, each of which is supposed to have a specific rôle (such an assumption is unwarranted and unjustified by the reality of generations); and second, the belief that a generation is an arithmetic quantity of thirty years. This view, which is merely chronological and biological, would indeed be quite arbitrary. Huizinga does not believe for a moment that generations correspond to genuine historical junctures based on the duration and disappearance of systems of *vigencias.* And as we might expect, his generalizations on how generations are to be interpreted turn out to be obviously inconsistent and deficient.

Spanish Reverberations

In recent years the topic of generations has been more widely discussed in Spain than in almost any other country and only in Germany has the theme been given as much attention. There are two reasons for this interest: the widely heralded "Genera-

61. J. Huizinga, "Problemas de historia de la cultura," *El concepto de la historia y otros ensayos* (Mexico, 1946), pp. 80–81. (Marías' italics).

tion of 1898," which has led to a general interest in defining generation as such; and the existence of Ortega's theory.

The designation "Generation of 1898" was introduced without any pretense of its being a precise term and without any reference to a generations theory. Gabriel Maura used the term first, followed by Azorín in 1910.[62] Since 1913 the designation of "1898" has become universal. In 1926, in a lecture entitled "Three Generations,"[63] Baroja drew attention to the "generations" of 1840, 1870, and 1900, but did little to clarify things. His criterion is the date of birth, and according to his scheme the second generation (1870) was his own—the one that was to be associated with 1898 by others. Frequent allusions to generations were also found in the writings of Unamuno.

With the appearance of the generations theory in Ortega's work, things become more complicated. In connection with his writings we encounter certain aspects of Spanish intellectual activity that might better be omitted were it not for the fact that they are symptomatic of other elements. Specifically, in recent years a certain pedantry has been evident in Spanish intellectual life. This tendency reflects a lack of real interest in problems that are properly intellectual, and is perhaps attributable in part to a desire for acclaim and an eagerness to appear blasé. The first thing certain critics do is to turn their eyes to Germany. Their underlying presupposition—and being presupposed, it is of course not stated—was this: "If Ortega can say these things, then think how much more must be known about them in Germany!" They immediately set out to see if this was true—not that they wish to acquire a clear understanding: they simply wish to be able to talk about it. But it turns out, as we have seen, that

62. Cf. Pedro Laín Entralgo, *La generación del noventa y ocho* (Madrid, 1945), p. 46.
63. Published in *Entretenimientos*.

considerably less is known about the question in Germany than in Spain. And so it is that hardly anyone has really gone deeply into Ortega's thought, with the unhappy result that little is known about his real position with respect to the generations theme.

It should be noted that the most serious item in this attitude toward Ortega is not hostility or ill-will; willful things are never excessively serious. The roots or the attitude are to be found in the social structure of our time. Intellectual frivolity and willful ignorance are the signs of the times. Pedro Laín Entralgo is a notable exception and the only one to deal seriously with the topic. He takes it up, as we shall see presently, not through caprice or faddishness but out of the requirements of his own work. This does not mean that everything in his book seems accurate to me, but it does mean that he has considered the concept with probity, insight, and mental effort, which is to say as an *intellectual*. The same cannot be said of other writers. We are confronted squarely with a social phenomenon—and herein lies its interest—that tells us a great deal about the very nature of the prevailing scientific attitudes; it is so deeply imbedded that it affects even extraordinarily gifted and often outstanding men, men who are admirable within the confines of their profession and among fellow specialists. In their pondering the problem of generations men of whom one would expect absolute precision and exactness are guilty of slips that they would consider unforgivable in their own professional specialty. No hostility should be read into my objections. In many cases these men are my very good friends, and in all cases they are writers of a caliber deserving attention. But the often-repeated saying attributed to Aristotle is appropriate here: "Amicus Plato, sed magis amica veritas" [Plato is a friend, but Truth is a greater friend]. With the generosity and cordiality that mark his character, Laín proposed a variation of this saying, which I make my own: "Amica veritas, sed etiam amicus Plato" [Truth is a friend, but Plato is just as much a friend]. And indeed when one likes and admires an intellectual one hopes for perfection in his work; this is what prompts my remarks.[64]

64. Were this anything other than a social problem, and were it not for a certain misfortune attached to the idea of generations, how could one understand how a great philologist like Dámaso Alonso, one of those men who have brought the most scientific precision and accuracy to the study of our literature, a man able to follow the thread of a verse from Sebastián de Córdoba to San Juan de la Cruz or to study with remarkable scrupulosity the *Soledades* of Góngora or *Versos plurimembres y poemas correlativos,* would allow himself to fall into error when he speaks of generations? In an essay entitled *Una generación poetica* (1920–1936), *Finisterre,* Tome I, Fasc. 3, (March, 1948), p. 197, Dámaso Alonso writes: "Can this be thought of as a generation? As a group? I make no attempt to define it. For more than a century deep German minds have been meditating on the differences and have come to no agreement." Is this true? We know that it is not. Not only, not even primarily, have the Germans been the ones studying the theme, but also those studies go back less than a century. But Dámaso Alonso does not stop with the scientific question, because here it is he who "goes apace" perhaps. Yet this is not quite true; beneath the poet in Dámaso Alonso lies always the philologist and professor. And the scholar in him will give us a bibliographical reference. Now how good are his references? We all know so very well; they are unsurpassed in exactitude. He gives us the original language, indicating the exact title, edition, date, page or line. For instance, he would say: "I shall in all cases refer to the following edition: *Rime di Luigi Groto, Cieco d'Hadria. Parte prima. A cui seguono altre due parti* . . . Venecia, 1610 (a copy of the work belonging to Gayangos, in the National Library, 3/26027–9). In the references to this work in the text, the Roman numeral indicates the *part;* the Arabic, the *folio."* Now then, the statement concerning generations in his work is followed by this note: "Concerning this problem, see the admirable book by Pedro Laín Entralgo, *Las generaciones en la Historia.* This work, together

Following Ortega, the next Spanish writer to delve at length into the problem of generations was Pedro Salinas. An admirable poet, Salinas is also a keen critic of our contemporary literature, which he has analyzed with matchless sensitivity and touch. In December, 1935, in a speech delivered at the P.E.N. Club, Salinas considered "The Concept of Literary Generation Applied to the Generation of 1898."[65] He admits that "these are only notes gathered from class lectures and are not a definitive edition nor an absolute point of view." Salinas alludes to the term "Generation of 1898," and adds: "More or less during the same years when this expression was being introduced in Spain by Azorín and the arguments concerning it were beginning, a notion of literary generations was developing in German literary science. It was conceived historically and generally at first, and then applied to the plastic arts and literature. From Dilthey in his *Essay on Novalis* (1865) to Jeschke (1935) there is a series of essays on the topic, among them the very enlightening works of Pinder, Wechssler, and Petersen, which treat the question of what constitutes a generation in literary history." He continues: "What I have tried to do in my courses is to see whether what Azorín called 'generation' through luck or fortunate intuition might correspond to the generation in German literary historiog-

with the essential essay by Ortega, are the greatest Spanish contributions to this much discussed theme." Aside from the fact that chronology would impose a reverse order, what is "the essential essay by Ortega"? Which writing is meant by this vague allusion? For the fact is that Ortega has written no essay on generations. There are many pages scattered throughout his work and two large sections of two books on the topic. Which text does Dámaso Alonso have in mind in advising the reader to consult it? (See Appendix 1 of this book).

65. *Revista de Occidente*, No. 150, Dec., 1935, pp. 249–59. Reprinted in *Literatura Española Siglo XX*. 2nd ed. (Mexico, 1949), pp. 26–33

raphy. In short, I have tried to introduce into the central polemic of whether or not there is a 'Generation of 1898' a conclusive judgment that will allow us to compare the literary facts of early twentieth-century Spain and the characteristics of a literary generation as defined by Petersen in his study *Literary Generations*." Salinas' debt to Petersen is obvious: he credits him with no less than the final word as to whether something may or may not be a generation and whether there really is a "Generation of 1898." But we have seen how fragile and inadequate Petersen's theory is, and moreover, how little merit there is in his very concept of "literary generation." At best it could serve only as an exemplification or abstract portion of a historical generation in its fullness. It is also surprising that Salinas does not turn to an older theory in his study of generations: the closer and incomparably more profound concept of Ortega. It is true that he dealt with Ortega's ideas in his university course at about the same time; and it is also true that Salinas was fully aware of the incomplete and provisional nature of these notes. But it is clear that his excessive attention to professional trends led him to exaggerate the importance of Petersen's study, and prevented him from seeing that the reality of generations can only be understood in terms of a general theory as distinct from minuscule intraliterary applications.[66]

66. A short time later, in 1936, Adolfo Salazar attempted to apply the idea of generations to the history of Romanticism, in particular to music. Referring only to Ernest Seillière's book, *Le Romantisme* (1925), Salazar uses the generation in the old genealogical interpretation and thus gives them a thirty-year interval. With this idea he tries to distinguish two Romantic musical generations, the second of which is divided into three stages. (Cf. *El siglo Romántico* [1936], pp. 16–17, and *La música en el siglo XX* [1936], pp. 21–25; 217–19). Salazar proposes alternating periods of three generations (thirty years in each) which he metaphorically calls

138

In a work entitled *Sobre sociedad e historia* [On Society and History], published late in 1939, José Gaos took up the problem of the generations.[67] He did not propose to treat the problem thematically, but to use the concept in considering a concrete historical question. This explains the brevity of his study and yet, as we might expect, the observations he does offer are precise and enlightening. He writes: "Generations appear as the building blocks of history. Lately, the doctrine or theory of generations has come to occupy an important place in philosophy and other disciplines, for example, in so-called literary science. The theme is central to the philosophy of Ortega y Gasset, who is perhaps the philosopher most responsible for its place of prominence; and it is from him that I take up the topic. But this is a theory that can be traced back to venerable antecedents. In one of the extant fragments of Heraclitus' work, the observation is made that 'a man can be a grandfather at thirty.' Ortega formulates generations on a fifteen-year scale. Even Homer speaks of human generations likening them to tree leaves (this certainly is not a modern view as we shall see). Ancient philosophy contained certain themes having to do with human life. These themes eventually disappeared (along with the very theme of human life as such) as philosophy was increasingly applied to other areas—extrahuman or abstractly human—such as physics or epistemological categories in modern philosophy. These ancient human themes reappear in the contemporary 'Philosophy of Life.' " Gaos goes on to examine several possibilities of what would happen, for example, *if* generations were individuals or a couple

"short centuries," and other periods of four generations which he terms "long centuries." For example, the seventeenth and nineteenth centuries were long; this leads him to expect that the twentieth will be "short."

67. Cf. José Gaos, *Filosofía de la filosofía e historia de la filosofía* (Mexico, 1947), pp. 135 ff.

of individuals, *if* there were only one generation (meaning that all men were coevals), *if* generations were "contiguous" at their beginning or end but not partially overlapping, or *if* they were all equal as in the case of animal or plant generations. He concludes that in all such cases there would be no history in any meaningful sense of the term. With this conclusion in mind, he turns his attention to a hypothesis that is foreign to our topic, namely, that there are portions of humanity lying outside of history (if we take history in the proper meaning). He states that there exist "human generations that are changeless and untouched by history." This seems to be a highly problematic notion indeed, despite Gaos's insistence on the evident appearances of such people as savages, fishermen, peasants, and shepherds.

There have been further soundings of the generations theory both in Spain and America in recent years. María Luisa Caturla, in a penetrating and suggestive book entitled *Arte de épocas inciertas* [The Art of Uncertain Periods] (1944), uses the generations concept in specific and opportune ways. She does this by summarizing Ortega's theory, along with references to Pinder and an allusion to Huizinga's observations.[68] She omits the philosophical bases of Ortega's theory and even the general theory, preferring to give her attention to a specific articulation of generations. Perhaps her most important contribution lies in pointing out and using Ortega's most explicit and mature works on the topic, and within the self-imposed limitations of the study she does this accurately.

A year later, in 1945, Alonso Zamora, a philologist and specialist in Spanish literature, attempted to apply the generations idea to a literary theme: lyrical Spanish poetry of the

68. María Luisa Caturla, *Arte de épocas inciertas,* (Madrid, 1945), pp. 151 ff.

140

sixteenth century. In "Sobre petrarquismo" [On Petrarchism], his inaugural speech at the University of Santiago, Zamora proposes to substitute a generational grouping of Spanish poets of that period for the traditional division between the Salamancan and Sevillan schools. He writes: "The attempt to write history according to generations appears in German historiology in the nineteenth century. Ranke and Dilthey took up the theme. Later, our Ortega and the German Petersen delved so deeply into the question as to show a generation's basic characteristics. Pedro Laín Entralgo's recent book contains a fine résumé of the history of the concept 'generation.' As for me, I shall adhere to Petersen's postulates, with an occasional reference to Ortega. I went into both theories quite deeply in a course at the University of Santiago de Compostela in the winter of 1944."[69] Zamora's work is a review or summary of the conclusions reached in that course, and the legacy of Petersen is quite apparent. The theory of generations, Zamora tells us, is German and begins with Ranke and Dilthey. He summarizes, very briefly, some of Ortega's ideas found in *The Modern Theme.* Yet he leaves out those in other works, although he cites *Esquema de las crisis* [Outline of Crises] (published in part in 1942 in *Man and Crisis,* which was also the name of Ortega's course, to which Zamora specifically refers) and states that he is familiar with one of the articles in *La Nación* [an Argentine newspaper] containing a portion of the same course, given in 1933 but still unpublished in book form. Despite this he adds: "Ortega's theory in reality is still lacking a systematic and broad study *by the author.*"[70] This seems more than passing strange if one considers the fact that my explanation of the theory in this book is based *exclusively* on texts

69. Alonso Zamora, *Sobre petrarquismo* (Santiago de Compostela, 1945), pp. 11–12.
70. Ibid., p. 11 (note).

published prior to Zamora's work; in most instances, indeed, I refer to the Ortegan titles just mentioned.

As for the rest of his work, Zamora, perhaps because of his concrete interest in groups of writers, underscores the *desire* for innovation and fame as a component of generations; among Ortega's ideas he inserts a statement alluding to the shaping influences of an individual life: "As it comes into being, a generation finds before it the models and norms imposed by the past. A writer coming to the fore wishes to add something to the past. He does not wish to pass by unknown in everyday language."[71] He goes on to recapitulate the eight generational characteristics according to Petersen and concludes: "From what has been pointed out, it can be deduced that the term 'generation' *does not mean a measure of regular time,* nor an equality determined by the date of birth, but rather a unit of existence, a similarity of life fixed by a common destiny. And this implies in turn a similarity of experiences and objectives. . . . The concept of generation thus explained *is of value only as a general guide, as a background on which are drawn historical changes."*[72]

In the second part of the book Zamora seeks to clarify the elements in the two generations of Spanish Petrarchists. In doing so, he adheres completely to their names and makes no attempt to specify the series of generations at that time. Nor does he even establish their connection with other coetaneous Spaniards. Therefore, the reason for the groups listed belonging to this or that generation is not given, unless it be the presence of some of the merely interindividual factors on Petersen's list. The length of these generations is not fixed. In the first one, the oldest name indicated, actually quite a bit older than the others, is Sá de Miranda (1481), and the last, Camões (1524). This means

71. Ibid., p. 13.
72. Ibid., pp. 20–21.

that between the first and last members of the generation there is a period of forty-three years. This exceeds, or rather triples, not only the span of a generation as Ortega saw it but also the period traditionally used by genealogists. If we leave out Sá de Miranda and begin with Garcilaso and Hurtado de Mendoza, the forty-three is reduced to twenty-one. Regarding the second generation, it begins with Ramírez Pagán (1525) and lasts at least until San Juan de la Cruz (1542), a seventeen-year difference. Taking as the terminal date 1524 of the first generation, and 1525 as the beginning of the second, we must assume an absolutely precise criterion as to the dividing line. But Zamora gives us no hint of what that criterion might be. We can see, then, how many problems would have to be solved before attempting such a rigid application of theory as is the case here. Furthermore, we should remember that the application attempted by Zamora in this work only nominally coincides with the historical method of generations.

A much more thoughtful attempt to deal with the problem of generations, in keeping with the nature of the work where it is found, is that of Francisco Ayala in the second volume of his *Tratado de Sociología* [Treatise on Sociology].[73] Ayala places the theme in a chapter dealing with "The structure of human life and its socio-historical articulation in generations." It is, then, in its rightful place. He refers to the analyses of human existence in Bergson, Heidegger, and Ortega, and he uses their results, especially Ortega's, in varying measure. But his adroit probing does not end here. He is aware of Comte's treatment of the topic, although he only cites one of Comte's less important passages, and he states that the generation is the "link on which is meshed the socio-historical process," and that in it is found "the basic

73. Francisco Ayala, *Tratado de Sociología,* Vol. 2: *Sistema de la Sociología* (Buenos Aires, 1947).

historical unit and, consequently, also the cardinal concept of Sociology." [74]

Ayala then examines the difficulties of a genealogical interpretation of generations and rejects it as an impossibility.[75] In doing so he turns to Ortega's theory. Referring to *Esquema de las crisis* [Outline of Crises], he says of that work: "Although unfinished, it is today the most complete study available for the problem of generations."[76] Now Ayala, without going into the philosophical foundation of the theory or the abstract or analytical theory of generations (the latter is the more serious omission), immediately sets out to identify specific fifteen-year generations. That is, he *begins* with what has yet to be touched on in the present study. It is rather surprising to discover this mistaken methodology in such an extensive, careful, and important work. Be that as it may, it is this mistaken approach that leads him into the difficulties that he proceeds to offer as objections to Ortega's theory. Properly understood, it is this same theory that resolves most of Ayala's objections. Ayala fails to see that selecting a particular figure such as Descartes as a point of departure in establishing the series of generations is but the first step in Ortega's method, and that *it is historical reality itself, not individual men, that determines the series.* But in order to show his objection and to reveal the deepest flaw in his thinking, we find him stating that: "Thus, for example, taking the year 1622 as a central point, the year when Descartes, who was born in 1592, reached thirty, we find that Bacon (born in 1560) belongs to the generation of 1577–1592; Galileo (born in 1564) to that of 1592–1607; while Richelieu (born in 1585) and Hobbes (born in 1588) both belong to that of 1607–1622."[77] He goes on to

74. Ibid., p. 152.
75. Ibid., pp. 153–55.
76. Ibid., p. 155.
77. Ibid., p. 156.

show the difficulties inherent in this division as well as the possibilities suggested by the selection of other men to mark a series.

Yet it happens that: (1) Descartes was not born in 1592 but in 1596 and so was thirty in 1626; this implies a completely different scale of generations and relationships; (2) neither was Bacon born in 1560, but in 1561; (3) the date selected by Ortega in each case is the *central* date of the generation, not the *final* one as Ayala seems to suppose (hence the generation is made up of the year selected, the seven preceding years, and the seven following); and (4) Ayala includes the same years (1592 and 1607) in *two* generations, which leads to nothing but persistent confusion. Moreover, the last two generations are sixteen years long. I am not easily disturbed or given to fretting unduly over a mistaken date *except* in the case of thought or even a criticism of a theory being based precisely on such dates! Carelessness of this sort, in a work of the scope and scientific value of Ayala's, is simply beyond understanding.

Aside from this weakness, Ayala has an accurate view of the significance of literary or artistic generations. They exemplify the general concept in specific, condensed, and more easily understood ways that permit a ready access to the topic. But the omission of the more substantial portions of the theory, prior to the details of its application, causes Ayala to skip over some of its fundamental aspects. He writes: "A generation cannot be defined as a sociological concept according to purely chronological criteria."[78] But it should be noted that historical chronology is never *pure* chronology, because dates point to historical realities and structures of collective life. Of course Ayala must add that "chronology is indispensable in fixing the concept of generation . . . a generation cannot be extended beyond certain rather narrow

78. Ibid., p. 157.

limits in time."[79] It is true also that he is aware of the weaknesses of Petersen's description of generations ("really not very brilliant").

This chronological vagueness in the idea of generation is due to the fact that Ayala does make sufficient and adequate use of the concept of "collective *vigencia*," and tends to consider things from the viewpoint of individual life. Despite the name, what Ayala calls the "social age" is really based on individual life and varies from period to period—even between closely connected periods—and from one social class to another.[80]

These are the most important Spanish repercussions and inquiries concerning the generation theory, from incidental but significant references, to detailed examinations falling within a doctrinal system.[81] We have yet to examine the work of Laín, which because of its scope and prominence deserves a separate treatment.

Pedro Laín Entralgo

The only Spaniard until now who has written a book on generations (not even Ortega has done so) is my excellent friend Pedro Laín Entralgo. Laín was led to consider the theme through the necessity imposed by his work as a historian. As early as 1944, in his book on Menéndez Pelayo, he touched on the subject and proposed a study of it. Through this book and other investigations into Spanish culture, Laín felt obliged to study the

79. Ibid., p. 158.
80. Ibid., p. 162.
81. A very brief but accurate discussion, with well chosen passages from Ortega's writings, is found in the *Diccionario de Filosofía* by José Ferrater Mora (2nd ed. [Mexico, 1944]) in the article on "Generación." (In the Fourth Edition, the article has been much improved and includes references to this book [Buenos Aires, 1958]).

Generation of 1898, about which he has written a huge and interesting volume. But before he was able to do this, he had to try to find out for himself the nature of generations. His research into this problem resulted in the book *Las generaciones en la historia* [Generations in History], published in 1945.

Of this book's seven chapters, the first five treat subjects that are, strictly speaking, preliminary to the theme itself: "Man's Dependence on History," "The Insecurity of Men," "Man's Escape from Himself," "Historical Creativity, Boredom, and Novelty," and "Biology and History: The Advent of Youth in Historical Life." Only the two final chapters are devoted to a treatment of generations, under the heading "The Generation as a Historiological Concept." Chapter 6 deals with a "History of the Concept." In it Laín alludes to the prescientific view of the generation and then he investigates the scientific period of thinking on the same topic. Besides mentioning Dromel and Cournot, Laín limits his history of the theme to the Germans—Ranke, Dilthey, Lorenz, Petersen, Pinder, Wechssler, Drerup, and Mannheim—and to Ortega. In the final chapter he poses several problems and sets forth his personal ideas.

Laín makes ample use of Ortega's writings in describing his doctrine, and his comments and summaries of Ortega's thinking are admirably precise. But he begins immediately with the theory itself without going into its general substructure. Hence one may take exception to his discussion of the "setting" of generations and consequently to the reality they imply. His main objection to Ortega is the latter's alleged biologism and vitalism: "Ortega's excessive historiological biologism is readily apparent. History is simply one among 'all the other biological disciplines.' "[82] Yet later we read: "although Ortega goes to an extreme in his biological interpretation of human ages, age is the doorway

82. Laín Entralgo, *Las generaciones en la historia*, p. 227.

through which one may enter into the Biology of History; it even becomes the 'reason' of history and is a peremptory influence in shaping it. His view of the rhythmic movement of generations as 'an automatic mechanism' is not an idle one. The primary element in the historiological thought of Ortega, as in all those who make of the generation the fundamental and basic concept of the historical process, is his radical vitalism. But history is the result of 'personal' acts, although these acts must be performed by some living person. For this reason the idea of a 'zone of dates' is not an empirical discovery, but a fabrication to support an *a priori* notion: the *a priori* assumption of 'vital' coetaneity of a generation and, in the logical extreme, of the biological conception of history. Had Ortega not thought that 'history is merely one of several biological disciplines,' as he tells us in *The Modern Theme*, most assuredly he would not have arrived at such an idea of the generation."[83]

Are these observations justified? I think not, for several reasons:

(1) Ortega informs us in *The Modern Theme*: "The terms 'biology' and 'biological' are used in this book, with special exceptions, to designate the science of life, understanding by 'life' a reality in which the differences between body and soul are secondary."[84]

(2) In the same book, after distinguishing between *zoé* and *bíos,* biological and bibliographical life, Ortega adds: "What Christianity prefers to this life is not lifeless existence but precisely the other life. That 'other' life can be any kind whatsoever, but it coincides with this one in the most fundamental feature: they are both life. The hope of the next life is biological in this

83. Ibid., p. 236 (note).
84. Ortega y Gasset, "El tema de nuestro tiempo," *Obras completas,* 3, p. 148.

one. *And when the day comes, and it is perhaps closer than the reader realizes, that a general concept of biology is formulated, in which traditional biology will be merely a chapter, celestial fauna and physiology will be studied and defined biologically, as one of many 'possible' forms of life.*"[85] We see, then, the nature of Ortega's biologism and how far removed it is from the mere physical body.

(3) Human ages, as we saw at some length, are not primarily a matter of biology, not ages of the organism, says Ortega, but of biographical life, or rôles and functions in this kind of life.

(4) The existence of an automatic mechanism is not the slightest proof of biologism in Ortega. Is it not also true that other such automatisms exist, for instance, those we call "social"? And must we exclude, on the other hand, the biological mechanism as a component of a nonbiological reality?

(5) Ortega wrote a long essay in 1924, the title of which is an expression of his thinking: *Ni vitalismo ni racionalismo* [Neither Vitalism nor Rationalism].

(6) Finally, it is true that the idea of a "zone of dates" is not an empirical discovery; but neither is it "a fabrication to support an *a priori* notion." Rather it is the content of an analytical theory, the meaning of which must be quite clear in order to understand the doctrine of generations. We see then that a lack of sufficient reflection on the theoretical structure of Ortega's thought has caused even Laín to be guilty of errors in his interpretation, despite the fact that in other respects his work displays consummate effort and magnificent intellectual qualities.

For Laín the origin of the idea of generation in the nineteenth century arises from a confusion between biological and personal life. He writes: "The generation, a period of man's biological life, was proclaimed the most elemental and idoneous unit,

85. Ibid., p. 189.

indeed the fundamental concept of historical life."[86] But this means that it is Laín who has a biological idea of generation, to the point that he will not admit that it could be something else. This explains his failure to see the extra-biological dimension of the generation, the dimension that is precisely the one appearing in history. And this is also why his astute observation that history cannot be equated with biology leads him to invalidate the very idea of generations. Within the same context he adds this paragraph, which I cannot read without some amazement: "With the same right granted the temporal span of a generation, the biological period of eating and digesting or the sleep-wake cycle could be considered for the lofty status as the measure and fundamental category of the historical flux. Nothing in the reality of things is disturbed by this line of thinking."[87] The reasons for selecting the generation as the basic unit, according to Laín, are its relative duration, the fact that it is more "coexistential" without ceasing to be biological, and the ease with which it allows a graceful structure to be fashioned from the contemporaneity of different ages. He concludes with these words: "Notwithstanding these exceptions, the intellectual trap remains. Whoever takes the generation as the elemental unit of historical change, and as the fundamental category of historical events, is exchanging with or without his knowledge, the true gold of historical and personal life for mere biological glitter."[88] Such immoderate and unjustified words are at odds with Laín's lofty prose, which we normally find combined with precision and serenity.

The upshot of all this is that the generation, in Laín's view, is not a historical category but a historical event that can be described as such. In a manifold sense—geographic, social,

86. Laín Entralgo, *Las generaciones en la historia,* p. 280.
87. Ibid., p. 280.
88. Ibid., p. 281.

chronological, thematic, and coexistential—a generation is radically "undefinable." Generations cannot be distinguished from one another by the nature of their life task but only by their manner of doing whatever they set out to do. Finally, Laín believes the style of a generation is similar to the personal habits of its members.

The reality of a generation cannot be rightly understood apart from the milieu in which it came into being. And without a theory of social and historical life, based in turn on an adequate philosophy, a theory of generations is an impossibility. Finally, such a theory is an absolute prerequisite for understanding generations in their unabstracted existence. The errors that may be imputed to Laín are traceable to a lack of these prerequisites; more than to the book itself—a book full of valuable and astute ideas—they point to something preceding the book. This case is an outstanding example, for in an intellectual of Laín's stature, so careful and punctilious in documenting his works, this deficiency arises from something prior to the investigation itself, from a deeply ingrained presupposition. It is apparent in his case that these previous notions have not received enough attention, and that they are deeply rooted in the social environment in which we live.

In this short review of the vicissitudes through which the generations theme has passed in this century, we are led to a perhaps unexpected conclusion: despite the great many writings on this problem that have appeared in Europe, Ortega's theory remains not only the first but also, strictly speaking, the only theory. And we should add that his theory has still not been completely understood in its entirety. Even less has it been used systematically. His theory is, then, intact and, in the literal meaning of the word, unknown. It is as if the theory had been conceived on Sirius or Alpha Centauri rather than in Madrid!

5

Problems
in the Theory
of Generations

AT THIS POINT, WE OUGHT TO LOOK BACK FOR A MOMENT
and contemplate the road stretching behind us from a fresh
perspective. At the beginning of this book we discovered the
generations theme to be an ancient discovery of human experience, but one that has only recently been seen as a "problem" to
be considered scientifically. Was it an archaeological bent that
led us to consider the hoary antecedents of the theme? Or was it
perhaps erudite curiosity? Actually it was something very much
the contrary: the proof of its reality. Today a theory of generations exists, yet generations themselves are not a theory but a
reality that men have come across quite apart from any theoretical concerns. For centuries they have manipulated the idea rather
crudely; today we consider it from another vantage point.

But we may well ask ourselves: is this merely a caprice? Was
the former "inaccuracy" truly insufficient for the time? On the
other hand, is our more precise view a superfluous luxury? We
must surpass the ingenuousness of rationalism and progressivism
and avoid the attitude of scientific *parvenus* that has typified
scientists, engineers, and medical men over the past two hundred
years. These men, so proud of their modern disciplines, usually

view the first steps of their sciences as lamentable and erroneous. It is interesting to note, however, that architects have been quite unable to fall into this error regarding the past, because of the high quality and structure of ancient buildings: the ancients erected buildings quite as good as ours. This fact should be kept in mind as one explores the technical capabilities of earlier men and ponders the ends that shaped their works. If they were better architects than engineers, is it not possible that they had no wish to be better engineers, and that they had no such wish because, in human terms, they did not feel the need to be? All knowledge must be interpreted in light of the situation in which the knowledge was felt to be needed. Thus, whatever the "imprecision" of man's thinking on the generation concept in earlier times, it was sufficient, given the life structures of the period and the nature of its relation to history. But in the last hundred years this relation has undergone changes of a magnitude unparalleled in former times. These changes are at once historical and extremely exact. As human life has experienced a radical alteration in the nature of its relationship to history, the generation theme has gone through the by no means minor vicissitude of becoming a scientific problem. This leads us necessarily to the conclusion that one of the things that has become a part of our experience is the generations theory. Stated in another way: luckily—and luck in such things cannot be counted on—the need for this theory has happened to coincide with the possibility of its existence.

Let us not forget that we began by raising questions about the players, the "actors" in the drama of historical life, and about the "unity of time," or elemental historical present. We need to know what generations are and to which generation we ourselves belong. Seeking answers to these questions, we first recounted the history of the idea in its most memorable periods. We did this not out of simple curiosity, and not out of scholarly zeal (which interests me not at all), but for three quite different reasons: (1)

because the story behind the idea forms the historical substance of the theme as such; (2) because this is one of the few examples in which we can be witnesses to the entire genesis of an important human discipline; and (3) because it is a visible and revealing example of certain structures of intellectual life during the last hundred years, and an example from which we may glean some highly important lessons.

Historical Reason

In charting the course of the topic of the generations in its chronological setting—that is, following the nineteenth-century attempts to formulate a theory—we have come across the only theory of generations in existence up to this point: that of Ortega. We saw that the date of his theory coincided in a remarkable way not only with the development of metaphysical and sociological postulates necessary for such a theory but also with the inexorable need for an adequate treatment of the concept. This was the very moment when the European had assimilated into his life the awareness of his historicity—initially, to be sure, in the misleading and hasty form of historicism. This was not so much a theory as the reality of what had actually happened to these men, though a theory might be derived from the experience. But an awareness of historicity and historicism itself are quite different things and should not be confused.

In a situation dominated by an awareness of historicity and historicist interpretation, the first precise theory of generations appeared. This theory was made possible by "historical reason." As an intellectual attitude, what is meant by this term? It is a form of reason destined for sailing deep waters, not for walking on solid ground and even less for finding one's way about a house, as the degenerate forms of reason are. It is a form of reason suitable for moving through the flowing, fluid, and plastic element of human life. To think according to historical reason is to embark on a voyage through an uncertain and unstable element. Most who set sail lose their bearings, accustomed as they are to confronting perils on a solid footing; they fail to realize that the accuracy of the instrument comes precisely from adapting to the moving plasticity of reality, as the boat adjusts to the rolling of the waves. This accounts for the fact that the philosophy of historical and vital reason is barely understood at all, and the fact that it usually produces sea sickness in men of the hinterland. They have never left the roadways of abstract reason, which is suitable only for traveling across the rigid surface of inert things.

But we must consider the other side of the question. In order to sail, in order to withstand and follow the flowing waves, a boat must have a rigid structure. This is the function of what we call the analytical or abstract theory of life and history. Though not enough for our needs, the theory is necessary. We cannot let it lie, because its purpose is to be filled with historical and concrete realities. In other words, we must launch the boat and navigate on the sea of life, for the boat only becomes a boat when it is afloat on the sea. Navigation bestows on the structure its reality as a boat. The general misunderstanding of Ortega's theory and the consequent unfruitfulness of both Spanish and foreign thought on the generations reflects the fact that some have remained within the mere scheme of the theory, like the hulk of a boat marooned on a beach, while others, perhaps the majority, have attempted to rely on purely empirical currents: they have set sail without a boat.

What We Know and What We Do Not

The steps we have taken so far become meaningful if we consider them all together: we know some things and are unaware of others. All these things have their place in the image we have formed of the entire theory as it has been presented. What do we know at this point?

First, we know that generations do exist, by virtue of the general structure of individual human life and of society or collective life.

Second, we know that several generations coexist at the same time: at any given date there are groups of men who are contemporaries but not coevals. Generations do not come and go in single file, but are overlapped, joined, and interlaced.[1]

Third, we know that the real course of history proceeds by generations, and that the several overlapping and coexisting generations constitute the intrinsically historical structure of society.

Fourth, we know that a generation lasts some fifteen years.

At this point we notice that the background has changed, that perhaps without being aware of it we have crossed a boundary of some kind. This fourth bit of knowledge seems to come from a different source than the rest. The first three statements do in fact spring from the abstract or analytical theory. Could the fourth statement, that a generation lasts some fifteen years, also be derived from that theory? Numbers are always somewhat strange and disturbing. One is not quite sure where they come from, or whether they are truly appropriate and not merely imposed on us. Even so, as numbers are also supremely comforting to many, they are quite happy to see them appear, and they rush out gladly to greet them, without noticing that on occasion, paradoxically, numbers introduce an essential vagueness.

This number fifteen should put us on our guard. It must be challenged and interrogated as to its origin. Have we crossed over the boundary of analytical theory into the province of history? If we consider this carefully, we will discern a third,

1. Mentré, who notices the phenomenon—though he does not interpret its meaning and consequences very well—offers the fortunate image of generations interlocked like "tiles on a roof."

intermediate zone having every appearance of legitimacy—a zone that might have escaped our notice, had we been careless. What we find, in effect, is an empirical datum, one that is not merely factual and based on chance but determined by the length of human life and the ages of that life. In other words, we find before us a constant—not, of course, a constant in the sense of the so-called "historical constants," but one analogous to Planck's "constants" or to the rate of acceleration of gravity at a certain point on the globe. In short, it is a datum arising from an empirical structure—empirical and yet a structure. This is not something that is merely contingent on other things, not a *factum,* in the sense that the Thirty Years War must last for that period of time to be meaningful, or that America had to be discovered in 1492 if the date is to make sense. Aristotle,[2] Porphyry,[3] and in imitation of them, the Scholastics all distinguished a third category between the "essential" and the "accidental," the category of that which is "proper" to man. It is *essential* to man, they said, to be rational; it is *accidental* that he be blond; and having two eyes and two feet, though neither essential nor accidental to man, is *proper* to him. But here we are dealing not with essences and accidents, nor hence with "properties," but rather with functional concepts that would belong to a logic of unabstracted thought. This logic has yet to be done, and alluding to the concept of what is "proper"[4] is at best a remotely analogous illustration.[5]

2. *Topics,* I, 5.
3. *Isagoge,* 5. True, Porphyry distinguishes between several meanings of the *idion,* and his interpretation does not agree with Aristotle's, but these differences are somewhat beside the point.
4. Cf. my *Introducción a la Filosofía,* Chapter 7, p. 61.
5. I have developed the theory of *empirical structure* pointed out here, in my essays, "La vida humana y su estructura empírica" and "La psiquiatría vista desde la filosofía," *Obras,* IV (*Ensayos de teoría* [Barcelona, 1954]).

The old way of thinking was inclined to attribute human things forthwith to a fixed mode of being called "nature." Leaving aside the problem of whether, in referring to man, one can speak intelligibly of a concept so misleading and equivocal as nature, it is clear that the great majority of characteristics commonly ascribed to nature are in fact historical and acquired. It happens that, rather than being passing qualities, they endure. They have been acquired, as was our custom of wearing a certain kind of tie, but the acquisition took place many centuries ago, perhaps before the farthest reaches of our historical knowledge. As an ideal and extreme case, it would be possible to have such characteristics affecting the whole of human history and yet be historical rather than "natural." The number fifteen, as the span of a generation, is generally valid, at least within broad historical boundaries. Later we must touch on points implied by this.

This is what we know; but we are still unsure as to what the specific generations are and to which of them we belong. This is an important point. We live our lives with the men of our generation and to a degree we are that generation. As we enter life, each of us is incorporated into a certain human stratum, into the section of society which is that of our coevals. These sections act as centers of social gravitation toward which individuals are drawn but in which we may find a special discontinuity between one center and another.

How are specific generations determined? Although our birth date implies that we belong to one or the other, the implication is not enough of itself. It tells us nothing about the scale of generations, and we continue to be unaware of whether our birth date places us in this generation or that one, and of whether we are at the beginning, middle, or end of a precise "zone of dates." To know the generation to which we belong, we need to know the established order of succession; only then can our birth date fall in place and acquire full meaning within a given generation.

Establishing the order of succession is by no means an easy

operation! We must not forget that generations are not juxta-posed but interlaced, and that at any moment several of them coexist. Hence, that commonplace question of the nineteenth century—just which generation is this one?—is quite meaning-less. We have to distinguish between two kinds of present time: (1) all generations living at a certain historical moment are present in the sense that they exist, but (2) only two of them are fully active and hence "present" in the fullest sense, whereas the others are either before or beyond this moment. Finally, a "pre-vailing" generation can be said to be the one in power or in the phase of full activity, and the one whose view of the world is predominant. The question now arises, how is the order of succession of generations to be determined?

Ortega's Procedure

"Consider," writes Ortega, "a great historical area within which a deep, evident, and unquestionable change in human life has occurred. In other words, let us begin with a historical moment when man was peacefully living secure in a certain world view. For example, we may take the year 1300, the time of Dante. Now if we consider the years following this date, we see clearly that European man is beginning to lose this comfortable attitude regarding his world. A little later on and we see that world begin to crumble and man unsure of the position to take. We continue and arrive at a time when man is again at rest with his world: he has once again entered a world of certitude where he lives complacently for centuries. . . . The Modern Age . . . transparently reveals the persistent and continuous development of certain life principles that were first defined at a particular date. Now this date is decisive in the succession of dates that make up the Modern Age. It marks the first time that a genera-tion lived with full understanding and perception of the new mode of thought. We find a generation that is neither forerunner nor heir. This is what I mean by a decisive generation. At the level of philosophical thought and science . . . there is no doubt whatsoever of when the full bloom of the new era occurs. It happens during the period of 1600 to 1650. Within this period the decisive generation must be isolated. To do this we seek the figure who most clearly represents the essential characteristics of the period. In our case, it seems beyond argument that this person is Descartes. . . . Hence we have found the 'eponym of the decisive generation,' and once this is done, the rest becomes mathematical routine. We note the date of Descartes' thirtieth birthday: 1626. This year would date Descartes' generation, becoming a point of departure from which other generations, before and after, could be fixed simply by adding or subtracting multiples of fifteen. . . . I have designated the years 1626, 1611, 1596, etc., as the dates of generations, not of persons. Only in the first case did we select as the date of a generation the thirtieth birthday of a particular man. If we accept the year 1626, then we can say that it is the center of a zone or cluster of dates corresponding to the temporal limits of the decisive generation. Therefore, those men of thirty as well as those seven years older or younger, would all belong to this generation. For instance, the philosopher Hobbes was born in 1588 and was thirty in 1618. Eight years separate him from Descartes. He is on the periphery of the 1626 generation; a year less and he would belong to it without question. Yet mathematically we must provisionally place him with the preceding generation."[6]

Such is the *modus operandi* proposed by Ortega in order to fix the "decisive generation" and with it the order of succession of the others. But is not this scheme excessively simple? Is it really anything more than arbitrary selection and unwarranted mecha-

6. Ortega y Gasset, "En torno a Galileo," *Obras completas,* V, pp. 51–52.

nistic manipulation? Ortega goes on to say: "What is meant by all this? Can it mean that mere mathematical routine, with its characteristic stupidity and abstraction, will decide historical reality itself? Not at all. This precise ordering of generations functions as an aiming device by which we approach historical data to see whether they can be ordered and adjusted according to this scheme. Suppose this were not so; let us imagine that Hobbes, by comparison to Descartes, should present the same vital profile and the same attitude before the intellectual problems of the world as Descartes. Then our system of generational succession would be erroneously articulated; we should have to review and revise the series of generations until the agreement of dates coincided with the real events of history, and until Hobbes belonged to the same generation as Descartes. But in point of fact, the case of Hobbes unequivocally confirms our proposed system."[7] Hobbes, according to Ortega, is on the borderline of the pre-Cartesian generation and the distance between the two is minimal. This can be seen in various matters; it is as though they both looked at the same landscape from close but different vantage points. Ortega adds that ". . . this difference in vital level is what I call a generation."

We have mentioned the more or less arbitrary selection of a central figure. But this does not mean that an individual imparts a tone to a generation and sets the scale for those that follow; for we can trace this tone and scale back to points predating such an individual. For instance, the structure of Descartes' world existed before he and his influence did. It is not the structure that is conditioned by the individual, but the individual by the structure. The generation "of" Descartes does not mean that it is a consequence of his life, that it is a generation defined by him, but rather the contrary; it is the generation to which Descartes

7. Ibid., pp. 52–53.

belongs. Of course, it is quite irrelevant whether the center of the decisive generation coincides with Descartes' thirtieth birthday. It is not necessary, and yet it is probably so. Hence this working hypothesis should be the starting point despite the possibility that the generational center might fall on Descartes' twenty-eighth or thirty-fourth year. Only history itself can decide this, only the *res gestae,* the empirical content of the human past, examined under the light that the concept of generation sheds on the past. It should be clearly understood that we are not speaking of similarities among men but of the world in which men live, of the structure of *vigencias* that make up the world of each man, of the problems arising from their world and their relationship to them. The last item should be stressed, for common problems do not arouse a common reaction; they affect the young, the mature, and the old in quite different ways.

We must examine at some length the process of determining generational succession within a specific historical time; only in this manner can the theory of generations become an effective historical method. But first we must put the theory itself to test. Several obections to it have been raised; we must gather them together and try to resolve them. Furthermore, we must raise some additional objections of our own that are possibly more urgent and subtle than those hitherto brought forth. In life it may be advisable to give credence to things without subjecting them to the most demanding of tests—after the example of Don Quijote when he took his mended helmet to be as good as new without putting it to a sword test. The only thing that cannot be so treated is a theory!

Objections to the Theory

The principal objections to the theory of generations can be grouped into six rather different categories:

I. The most radical objection to the theory of generations

consists in simply denying the concept—denying, that is, the very existence of generations as such. This objection, in turn, involves two kinds of difficulties:

(a) The concept of continuous occurrence.

(b) The reduction of the concept of generation to a limited human group, which makes it possible to believe that:

1) the movement of history is as continuous as the succession of births, and changes occur in imperceptible transitions of no fixed pattern; or 2) a "generation" is no more than a certain class of affinities between individuals in a given place and time. This is what is usually understood, for instance in Spain, by the "Generation of 1898," a group of well-known writers.

In both cases the answer is the idea of *vigencia*—not biological continuity but rather the abiding structure of a social form or system of *vigencias*. In other words, it is the life span of a certain kind of world. This life of the total system, which determines the mode of historical changes, does not exclude, to be sure, continual *partial* changes. The key to the problem is the distinction that Ortega makes between changes *in* the world and changes *of* the world itself. A given change may be quite important but it occurs in a world that is itself unchanging; it is incorporated into the same world, which by definition continues unchanged.

Moreover, this prevailing world style includes all who live in the world. The peculiarity of certain groups of individuals only affects partial and for the most part superficial zones. Differences exist between groups of the same generation, and these differences, because they affect ideas and the notions that men utter, are usually quite noticeable; even so, they hardly touch what is deeper and more common to the men of a generation: their beliefs—an area of life that lies largely unnoticed and unspoken and perhaps even unknown.

II. Analytical considerations reveal the need for some idea of generations, even though their empirical reality may be unknown to us. On the borderline between abstract analysis and history we find the quantitative positing of a generation as a period of fifteen years. The second general objection to the generation theory is to deny the truth of this specific length of time. But, in turn, this general objection may be divided into three smaller but distinct ones: (a) There are no fixed rhythms or invariable periods, (b) a generation lasts not fifteen but thirty years, and (c) why should a generation be *exactly* fifteen years long? Let us examine each of these three objections separately, in order to see whether they are justified or unfounded.

(a) *There are no fixed rhythms or invariable periods.* This is the notion that there are no generations except at certain times, in certain types of societies, in very crucial times, or when important historical innovations occur. For instance, there was a generation—or generations—of reformers in the sixteenth century; there were other generations responsible for the French Revolution; still others during the Romantic period; and the Generation of 1898. This idea of generation is more or less openly stated in many books. At the very least, generations of this kind would be "concentrations" of historical activity associated with more or less illustrious groups. Expressed in different ways, this was the idea of Pinder and Petersen, among others.

But there must be a rhythm in human things, because human life has a fairly constant average length and a structure consisting of an invariable sequence of ages. This is not only, or even principally, a question of biological rhythm but rather one of the *social* functions of successive age groups. The important point is the existence of a phase of social preparation before historical participation, another phase of participation or activity, another of retiring from the historical scene. Imagine a man of extraordinary longevity in full control of his faculties: he would be unable to continue indefinitely in a single life stage or phase and would have to continue inventing new "ages" or styles of life, and new social functions. Furthermore, the condition of generations does not stem from "important" historical events; supposing this to be so is the error that has crept into the hackneyed notion of a "Generation of 1898," which over the years has been emended and corrected. Historical events, "important" or otherwise, are lived and experienced in different ways, depending on the viewpoint of each generation involved. A similar thing happens with events in personal life: losing one's parents, falling in love, getting rich or going bankrupt, becoming famous—all happen at different ages and have a different meaning accordingly. Age lends meaning to events rather than being shaped by them.

(b) *A generation lasts not fifteen but thirty years.* This is the objection based on genealogy, the thirty-year period based on the biological relationship between parent and child. But we have seen that genealogy cannot really be the basis of generations because of the continuity of births (which becomes decisive if we consider biology alone, ignoring the idea of social *vigencia*) and the age difference between the children of the same father. But it is also possible to propose the number thirty for socio-historical reasons, if we consider thirty years to be the average duration of man's mature activity. However, the mere fact that this thirty-year span is divided into two diametrically opposite phases that are joined in contention with each other—preparation and accomplishment, the struggle for power and the exercise of it—is enough to make us realize that the *vigencia,* the predominance of a generation, lasts for only half of its entire historical presence.

(c) *Why should a generation be* exactly *fifteen years long?* The exactness of the number fifteen stirs a certain uneasiness. Why this number and not another? Is such quantitative precision permissible in things human? Does this not present an unwarranted arithmetical abstraction that reminds us of biology, or even more of astrology? Let us look closer. Of course, the duration of a generation must be very close to fifteen years, because it is at about the age of fifteen that we leave childhood, and about the age of thirty that we begin our participation in historical events. This phase of activity lasts for about thirty years and is in turn divided into the two sub-periods already discussed. After the age of sixty the decrease in the number of survivors is considerable, and those who are left enter retirement (at least this was true until recently). We are dealing, then, with a quantitative component in the concept of generation, but a component that strictly speaking is also a quality of life. In human affairs it is not arithmetic quantity that imposes exactitude. For example, every individual has a certain height and weight. What may these be? They are not restricted to a set figure but neither can they be unlimited: a man cannot be thirty feet tall and weigh a thousand pounds or an inch tall and an ounce in weight. Now, the number fifteen acts as a round number; another number close to it would force us to accept it as an *exact* number. As a number that distinctly *excludes* mathematical exactitude we must necessarily accept the figure of fifteen. And yet we do not have to accept it rigidly; the empirical reality of history *could* show some variation from this mean, however small. On the other hand, the fifteen-year span suggests itself methodologically and we should not readily reject it. If experience were to oblige us to change our view, we should do so, of course, but only after making pertinent attempts to resolve the difficulties without changing the number. In no case would changes be made based on problems of placing a single individual within a generation, but on *structural*—that is, world—problems.

The foregoing are the two principal objections to the generations theory. They refer to the existence and consistency of generations. Now let us examine some others within the theory itself and hence of lesser scope:

III. What about women in such a theory? Up to now we have

said nothing about the division of humanity into two sexes. We must hasten to remedy this simplification of method, which amputates a decisive dimension of human reality. Do women cause some disturbance in the generations theory—it would come as no surprise if they did—aside from a certain customary manipulation of the "numerical datum" in question, which might create some problem in applying the theory? Do women belong to the same generation as men of the same age?

The greater precociousness of woman and her earlier debut into mature life would suggest a negative response to this question. Ortega noted in passing that ". . . the women of a generation essentially and not by chance are a little younger than the men of the same generation; this fact is more important than it first appears."[8] It would be necessary, for a precise answer, to determine by means of exact empirical investigation the age differential of men and women in the same generation, stressing whether this difference is fixed or variable. For possibly this discrepancy could decrease or even disappear when the forms of social life rectify this biological precociousness. We must remember that the mechanism of generations is social in nature. Thus, in our time, the insistence of women on adolescent modes, including their prolonged childhood (quite apart from a partial "precociousness" that is in any case common to both sexes and is merely superficial), their backwardness in certain areas that require schooling paralleling that of men, their participation in the same kind of work as men, the lateness of marriage, and the frequency of marriage with men of the same age, etc., are all factors that strongly point to a chronological leveling of feminine generations.

IV. Which people are affected by a generation? Which are included? It is absurd to think that it is a little group of friends, a

8. Ibid., p. 4.

gathering in a café, or the collaborators in the publication of a review. But does a generation include everyone? Does it comprehend a thirteenth-century European and an American Indian of the same period? Evidently not. Generations display a unitary character within the same "historical units," which is to say in societies, that are in communication and not merely aware of one another. Europe is a historical unit today, and it has been for some time, because all its parts are effectively in communication. But it would be impossible to establish a unity of generations between Europe and China, because the system of *vigencias* is different in the two societies. Even so, we must keep in mind that humanity is not dispersed around the world in eternally fixed ways and with constant relationships and distances. Rather we find continuous change and variation of societies internally and with respect to each other. Two isolated or barely connected units of civilization may develop a real communication; or a small unit, hitherto independent, may be incorporated into a larger whole. The course of generations in these critical phases may undergo decisive vicissitudes. To use a fluvial image unbelied by human reality (as Jorge Manrique is my witness), one may say that there are human "main streams," other groups that are "tributaries," and in still other cases unions of two or more "confluences." The important element is always the *vigencia*. A society's system of *vigencias* is received when a group really belongs to it; that is what regulates the scale of generations.

Is all of humanity, albeit perhaps in different groups, subject to the rhythm of generations? We recall that Gaos spoke of societies "at the peripheries of history" (primitive peoples, for instance, and certain rural groups). These societies would repeat the same forms of life endlessly and would undergo no change. Thus, all generations would be *equal,* and from the socio-historical point of view, though not the genealogical, there would in fact be no generations as such. Still, let us remember that we are speaking of *how* changes occur and *how deep* they are. If we hurl a stone into the middle of a lake, waves spread in diminishing size throughout the water, and wave motion is maintained all the way to the outer edges. Similarly, we should find centers of maximum historical change and primitive or rural peripheries of slighter variation. Nevertheless, all societies experience change, whatever the intensity, according to the rhythm of generations.

V. There is the problem of abstract units within a generation. Does one belong to different generations in different life dimensions? Is there one series for literature, another for politics, and still others for painting, science, and love? We must remember, as John Stuart Mill noted in 1843 and as I have not wearied of repeating, that the generation has a total character. Abstract dimensions of it cannot be isolated except as unreal procedural simplifications. There is only one scale of generations and this affects life in its entirety. It is possible that a partial society, such as a nation, may exhibit a certain "backwardness" in some specific aspect with respect to the larger society of which it is a part. While the succession of generations is tied to the larger society, the "backwardness" becomes a part of the structure of the sub-society. Perhaps Spanish literature of the Romantic period is a generation later than the central European trends. By this I mean that the first Romantic generation in Spain, Romantic in all areas of life, would create a literature *still* not Romantic, while a generation would follow that was fully Romantic in its literature but no longer so in real life. This explains the possibility that within the same historical community, and therefore within the same series of generations, "echelons" may be formed between different countries. Thus some would be more or less "advanced" or "backward" in science or art; that is, some would be the innovators, and others the followers or passive recipients.

VI. We must consider also the problems of individuals, and these are legion. For instance, we find the man who lives in abnormal circumstances because of illness or other causes, and who enters the world late. The extreme case of this would be Segismundo (protagonist in Calderon's *La vida es sueño*), for whom the historical world would have immediately coincided with the "system of *vigencias*" revealed to him by Clotaldo, his teacher. Or we find men attracted to past generations and who feel they are *revenants*. Then there is the distortion of "social age"; just as psychologists speak of "mental age," so one might well conceive of a "social age" to signify the image that, from the viewpoint of age, a public figure—writer, artist, or politician—presents to his contemporaries. Now then, when a man asserts himself early in life, or when his activities are superior to what is normal for his age, he seems to others by virtue of his fame or importance, the "equal" of older men. In these cases, the younger man is granted the same esteem, or at least is thought to be as important, by his contemporaries as older men. He associates with the older generation, although he does not really belong to it. From the individual point of view, this exemplifies the rôle of elite minorities within the arena of whole generations.

In outline form, the foregoing are some of the more important objections that can be raised against the theory of generations. As we have seen, however, the theory itself answers these doubts and even seems the clearer and the more genuine for having done so. This is because the theory of generations reveals itself procedurally; that is, it has to be applied to historical reality in order to become fully realized as a theory. Far from being a structure that is ill-fitted to be imposed on reality, it depends on reality for its final accuracy. And it is reality itself that forces the theory to justify itself—completing and developing itself in the process—in terms of its problems, difficulties, and deficiencies. As we shall shortly see, the theory of generations is intrinsically procedural and practical.

6

The Historical Method

THE THEORY OF GENERATIONS CLAIMS TO BE A KNOWL-
edge of reality and as such it cannot rest tranquilly on itself. It is
presented as an analytical theory whose aspects imply an empirical application. It can reach its full theoretical effectiveness only
when it functions circumstantially in apprehending historical
reality. Hence my reference to the theory of generations as being
intrinsically procedural or methodical in nature: its application is
not merely consecutive or consequential, but is rather the very
means by which the theory itself is fulfilled. It is our task, then,
to set forth clearly the manner in which a succession of generations in a given period and place is to be investigated.

Generational Series

We need to find firm footing regarding the generation to
which each of us belongs. We know with certainty only that
those of us who were born in the same year belong to the same
generation, and that those born fifteen years earlier or later
belong to one or the other of two contiguous generations. Of the
intermediate dates we can assume nothing at this point nor can
we as long as we are unaware of the order of succession of the

generations in question. In other words, our knowledge is extremely limited until we are able to transcend individual life and enter the realm of collective life structures. For in fact, since I do not know the level at which I was born into my generation—and this because I am unaware of the order of succession between it and others and hence cannot know its boundaries—neither can I know whether there is not perhaps some "great divide," some generational boundary, lying between my birthdate and another man's. In short, we cannot be sure at this juncture whether we belong to different generations (though these might be separated only by a short temporal distance) or to the same generation (though as many as fourteen years may separate us).

With a person known by me personally I have the impression that he is either "of my time" or, alternately, that he is not; I coexist coetaneously with some men and not with others. In this way, and almost without being aware of it, we make a subjective outline of generations. This is not an outline of dates but of proper names: this person seems to belong to my generation, another, to a previous period, and still others, to more recent generations. It would be possible, and indeed of some value, to attempt an empirical description of generations, basing it on the birthdate and proceeding thence to reveal its chronological delineation. But aside from requiring a sufficient number of examples to work with, great care would have to be exercised so as not to confuse the real but subjective impression that certain people "belong to my generation," when in reality they merely share an affinity of ideas, opinions, and affections that have little or nothing to do with the generation itself.

Besides, resorting to this would be a mere heuristic expedient that would lead to an attempt to justify our connection to these respective generations, rooting the justification in the objective structure of the *vigencias* of the supposed generations. At best it would be a guiding principle in understanding our time. But all the while the proper perspective would continue to be lacking. In no case could it be a general historical method, because, aside from its inadequacies in justifying even our own time, it could not be applied to former periods.

We may consider a generation to be a historical orbit or circle situated within an attractive environment. As a man enters life he is attracted to a certain social center of gravity and is eventually incorporated into a nucleus constituted of people generally younger or older than he. The age group depends on whether his birth falls near the beginning or end of the "zone of dates" by which his generation is circumscribed. Two men of nearly the same age may gravitate toward different social groups, one joining a younger group, the other an older. The reason for this is that, despite the temporal proximity of the two men, they are separated by a generational demarcation line. Thus, each will feel that he is with men of his own age (using the term "age" in the socio-historical sense) even though age differences within each group are often greater than that between the two men in question.

How may the succession of generations be objectively determined? Let us recall the brief guidelines laid down by Ortega: discovering a "decisive" or "critical" generation, identifying its "eponym," setting up a provisional hypothetical scale as a vehicle to guide us into historical reality, and taking the thirtieth year of the eponym as the center of a generation (the birthday of such a man would yield the same result, since from birth to the thirtieth birthday there are exactly two generations). With this outline we have only begun, of course, for only an empirical consideration of historical reality itself can confirm, rectify, and definitively fix this scale. Moreover, it is not always easy to locate the "decisive" generation: long stretches of history are critical and clouded. Nor can we in all cases readily spot a representative figure in, for instance, the "dull" periods mentioned by Ortega. In these circumstances, therefore, we must find complementary methods in our search for a precise delineation of generational succession.

Nothing we might say about individual lives would be enough. For it to be we would have to transcend the structure of the collective *vigencias*. Let us suppose we are inquiring into the present age in order to ascertain what is happening in the world. The diversity of present generations reveals at least three worlds we must consider: the world of today's youth, that of the mature man, and that of the aged. Without specifying which of these generations is meant, in the deepest sense, we cannot know what is happening, for we do not know to whom it is happening, nor in which social group any particular individual lives. Life and history are systematic in their structure, and there are essential relationships between private and collective life that are expressed in the form of generations. Yet we still do not know exactly to which generations we refer. How shall we come to know them?

We recall that Descartes, feeling himself lost in a sea of doubts, clung to doubt itself as the only substantial thing on which to construct his philosophy and thus surpass doubt. Let us proceed in the same way, beginning with our very ignorance of the generations we wish to ascertain.

If we take a series of representative figures born fifteen years apart, we have a list of "representatives" of at least several generations. We do not know which generations these are exactly, for we cannot yet set their boundaries. All we know is that no two men on the list belong to the same generation, and that all of them belong to connected and successive generations. In other words, every generation in the entire period is present and represented. Stated in another way, the generations are still unknown, but their representatives are not; and in these representatives, as individual men, the differences in level or historical plane that mark the generations are revealed. As we add other names to the list, the names of men who unquestionably belong with those already listed (either because they were born in or about the same year or because they display the essentially same attitudes to the problems of the time), the series becomes richer and fuller. Each generation is represented no longer by a single man and year but by groups of names covering a "zone of dates" still more restricted than the entire and as-yet-undefined generation. This group represents a nucleus or portion of the total generation. As a better illustration, I shall demonstrate this method with some names, confining myself to Spain in the interest of simplicity.

If we select at random—we shall admit no special dates as yet —the year 1809 as our starting point, the succeeding generations would be marked by the years 1824, 1839, 1854, 1869, 1884, and 1899. Now, if we group the names of men born on or within two years of these dates, we have a series of names that belong to the seven generations in question (the boundaries of which, I repeat, are still unclear):

> *First Generation:* Espronceda, Cabanyes, Larra, Donoso Cortés, Gayangos, O'Donnell, Balmes.
> *Second Generation:* Carolina Coronado, Roque Barcia, Valera, Pi y Margall, Sagasta, Eulogio Florentino Sanz.
> *Third Generation:* Fortuny, Ricardo de la Vega, Salmerón, Giner de los Ríos, Gumersindo de Azcárate, Laverde.
> *Fourth Generation:* Maura, J. O. Picón, Palacio Valdés, Canalejas, Rodríguez Marín.
> *Fifth Generation:* Granados, Menéndez Pidal, Primo de Rivera, Besteiro, Gabriel y Galán, Gómez Moreno, Zuloaga.
> *Sixth Generation:* Ortega, Américo Castro, Onís.
> *Seventh Generation:* Zubiri, Dámaso Alonso, García Lorca, Enrique Lafuente.

Thus we would proceed, going into greater and greater detail, and increasing the range of our scrutiny. The dividing line between generations would be found somewhere between these successive clusters of dates. In diagram form, if we designate the beginning point as year 0, and mark the names corresponding to each group or nucleus of a generation with an identical letter and a certain number of apostrophes, we will have:

Year 0: A, A′, A″, A‴, etc.
Year 15: B, B′, B″, B‴, etc.
Year 30: C, C′, C″, C‴, etc.
Year 45: D, D′, D″, D‴, etc.

As we proceed in this way, the uncertain zones will become quite restricted. Even so, the final word could not be found in individual lives, not even by way of this orderly accumulation of data, but rather only in public life and in collective *vigencias*. Earlier we saw the necessity of generations in determining the structure of collective life at a given moment, the reason being that public life is fashioned by the interplay of *vigencias,* which are the subject of whatever is occurring in society at the moment. Now, on the other hand, we find that we need to know the social *vigencias* in order to determine the succession of generations. It appears to be a vicious circle.

A circle, yes, but perhaps not a vicious one. What we find is perhaps an especially visible manifestation of the structure of historical reality: its system. Hence the need to turn to our earlier expedient of representative figures in order to deal with generations without knowing exactly which ones we are treating. This allows us to organize our search for their definition. What does this mean exactly? It means that although I cannot readily identify the generations, I do have a series of representatives of them—concrete representatives of hypothetical generations, as it were. Thus, I can uncover the repertory of *vigencias* through the respective representatives, and thereby measure the variation between one generation and another. In this I obtain a profile of each generation and the differences between them. Once I have these general profiles, I compare them—not the individual men —with all specific and individual reality known to me. And this reality will be seen to sort itself into one or the other of these profiles. By means of this methodical procedure, the reality under my scrutiny gradually comes into sharp focus so that every item can be accounted for. In other words, men born at any time during the period can now be ascribed to a specific generation for reasons that derive from collective life. Similarly, the boundaries of generations can be fixed, allowing the true scale of generations during a certain period to be firmly established.

A highly mechanistic (with the advantages that could have) operating procedure for locating the dividing line between generations would consist of taking the series of representative years that I have just explained, together with their corresponding names, and matching throughout the series the years close to the respective names. Very likely these contiguous dates would belong to the same generation as the starting year. This procees would continue until anomalies appeared in comparing a given date with the earlier ones. This would have no significance and would be irrelevant in the case of individual and isolated difficulties. But if these anomalies could be observed at the same level throughout the series and in each generation, we could take the anomalies to be an indication that we had reached a dividing line, or in reality a series of them, between generations. Turning again to the earlier outline, for example, if after adding successively four years to the years 0, 15, 30, 45, etc., and incorporating these years into generations A, B, C, D, etc., we find anomalies appearing when we add the fifth year throughout the series, then the dividing line of generations A, B, C, D, would be fixed at the years $0 + 4$, $15 + 4$, $30 + 4$, and $45 + 4$. The year $0 + 5$ would become, on the other hand, the first year of generation B, and so on successively. This procedure, whose principle is none other than the theory earlier expressed, can be reduced to mechanical routine of the sort indicated, and be quite useful in dealing with long series and a large enough number of names to complete and confirm the results of the method.

Yet not even all this is enough. History is a highly complex reality. Its methods require us to adapt ourselves to the rich multiplicity of its ingredients and the real connections among them. How can we investigate the diverse structures of the collective world so as to situate the individuals of a period in their rightful place within these structures? Let us consider the possible forms of experiencing a historical innovation, that is, a distinctively new form of life, whether this form be the reformist attitude of the sixteenth century, the Rationalism of the seventeenth, or the Romanticism or democracy of the nineteenth. Suppose that we have an innovation that spreads quickly throughout an entire society. We may discount its possible delay in affecting certain rather closed minority circles. Think, for example, of how long it took for Hellenization to become a social fact for the Romans (even with their elite minorities) after it had been introduced by certain identifiable groups, or of how long it took for the Copernican theory to become the historical reality of Copernicanism. This is why I consider that each of the forms of experiencing an innovation of this type coincides with a generation. We must also take into account, however, the fact that in other cases a slower and more complicated mechanism for transmitting and spreading the innovation would require two or more generations for each step. In such cases, a generation would correspond to a phase of the transformation. The sequence of forms would then be as follows:

(1) Initially the innovation is individual: a youthful minority proposes a new life style and struggles to impose it on a world of a different persuasion. These men live their lives in an effort to convert the whole of life to a new vital sensitivity. When they reach maturity, their purpose reaches its first phase of prevalence.

This is the first generation in a period—the creative and initiating generation.

(2) The second generation receives, at the outset, the forms created by the previous generation. These forms now have a social existence. The world in which the second generation happens to live displays a structure, albeit a very tenuous one, suited to their common personal aims. These men are already to a minimal degree heirs to an attitude they did not create but on which they base their personal aims. Other men performed the first deeds arising from this new attitude; the second generation repeats them more energetically, though perhaps not without some reservations, inasmuch as the attitude has already begun to lose some of its early magic. The men of the second generation begin to *know* that they are rationalists, romantics, or democrats, and often we find them deliberately fabricating a stereotyped personality for themselves—one defined by the tastes, demands, and requirements of the basic program implied by the new life form. We also discover in them a smug group-consciousness in their attitude towards others whom they consider backward because they are not part of their world. Such men know what they are and they cling to this awareness; their predecessors, the men of the first generation, were simply what they were without knowing it.

(3) The third generation has little or no need to create. When it becomes aware of the world in which it finds itself, it sees that this world has a fixed and established structure. Stated in another way, the new life form has now reached the level of a social *vigencia*. Two symptoms are usually associated with the phenomenon: men begin to reflect and theorize on the attitude in question, and they begin to refer to it in ironic terms. Aside from these symptoms, it is this generation that, on the surface, most eminently fulfills the promise of the "new" form of life. The most "representative" figures nearly always are found here.

But we must remember that what is representative is seldom what is most authentic. This is a generation of "heirs" who have begun to live within a tradition. Once established in this tradition, and with a wealth of beliefs that generally support it, the heirs begin to test new attitudes. The ease that has marked their life, their not having felt any need to innovate and struggle with their surroundings, allows them to begin seeing the limitations of this way of life. As a consequence, the basic beliefs on which the society has by now become firmly founded begin to weaken gradually and to rupture in certain individuals.

(4) The fourth generation, finally, no longer fully belongs to the life form in question. These men still live more or less within the system, to be sure, but in the recesses of their being they are unable to reconcile their calling to its style. In a certain way, their situation is just the reverse of the first generation. While the latter was itself something new, its world was not; the fourth generation, on the other hand, is no longer sincerely a part of the world in which it lives, but the world itself continues along in the now outdated attitude. What the men of the fourth generation have inherited, the elements that form the social being of each of them, is the repertory of customs, forms, and beliefs created and confirmed by the three preceding generations. But while such is their past, their future is something else; they have other aims, they go toward things different from those whence they came. Thus, we discover necessarily among the members of the fourth generation either a transition to new forms or a hollow insistence on the past. The latter is simply an affectation.

Now then, in periods of outstanding historical innovation or change—the periods that lend themselves most readily to an investigation of the problem of generational sequence—it is not difficult to discover in which of these four situations an individual is to be placed with respect to the new life form. A careful study of this kind would permit us to bring the generations into clearer focus and to see their order of succession. This is in keeping with the empirical nature of the theory, which must always be amended according to facts.

We have seen something of the careful and difficult investigation needed to apply the generation method to historical reality. Without a preliminary outline of the generations of a period, its world structure eludes us. On the other hand, without an analytical theory of human life, both collective and individual, the real succession of generations cannot be determined. Failure to master these fundamental problems has led more than one writer into nebulous and baseless conjecture, while others, more keenly aware of their intellectual responsibility, have become disappointed with a method that is only effective when fully applied.

A View of History

Let us try, finally, to understand the view of history when seen through this new focusing instrument of generational scale. What is the form of historical reality as viewed in terms of the generations that continually coexist and replace each other?

We should first recall the usual image of history. We find two possibilities: (1) the fragmentation of history into historical events and happenings; and (2) the morphology or description of cultures.

In the first case, the things described are really unintelligible, because we begin by knowing neither to whom the events described happened nor who experienced what is said to have occurred. The only thing we know without doubt is that the historical event, and precisely to the degree that it is historical, does not happen to the "protagonist." For instance, the English Revolution did not happen to Cromwell, though in a certain sense he can be said to have "executed" it and he was deeply affected by it personally. Still, it is evident that he was not the real *subject* of these events, and to say that England was the subject is to exaggerate, or still worse, to be excessively vague. The essence of a historical fact can only be understood when it is referred to a total situation that is greater than both its "facts" and the sum of them all. The real meaning is not to be obtained through a mere accumulation of events. The ideal of the historian in search of materials for the study of a period would be to have at his disposal what newspapers offer us concerning our own: all the facts of any importance reported fully and commented upon. But it so happens that this historian could not possibly understand the mass of countless preserved facts. In our case, we understand the newspapers because we have an idea of the structure or life form of our time. And even when we have arrived at this idea without the benefit of any scientific or intellectual effort, it enables us to classify automatically the items of news that the daily press serves up with our breakfast. But how well do we understand even these facts? It is a well-known truth, although many refuse to see the gravity of the matter, that political news from foreign countries is generally misunderstood except by those familiar with the countries. Party names, political slogans, what people are saying—all remain ambiguous so long as there is no clear notion of the total reality to which these partial elements pertain. I recall reading a German newspaper in 1935 and coming across an article dealing with Spanish politics. I encountered the expression *Erneuerungsbewegung.* It required some effort for me to realize they were referring to the "Spanish Renovation" or "Renewal," and I found myself imagining the gulf between the experience the German reader would have on seeing this, and the impression the corresponding term would have on the Spaniard. History books are usually something less than history; instead of history they offer only materials, and these without elaboration. It devolves on the reader to make his own version of history. This he nearly always does—and with perfect right—rather poorly. He enmeshes the data served him in the name of history in a vague sense or notion of life, which for better or worse he may have derived from a Romantic play or from a novel by Alexander Dumas. Even so, it does let him understand history in a limited way, for it gives him a setting—however fictitious and devoid of elements—in which he can situate the facts offered up by the historian. This explains the frightful boredom of history textbooks, the student's distress in studying them, and the incredible ease with which everything in them is forgotten. Conventional history texts, for the most part, are not intelligible and do not allow us to enter them through imagination so as to relive their content. In contrast, I vividly remember, after almost twenty-five years, the books of Moreno Espinosa, which though without scientific value or precision, had been annotated by my old professor Don Francisco Morán. These were books filled with delightful, lively, and amusing items. They contained anecdotes, poetry, stories, and gossip—the simplest guides to reliving the past. It should not be forgotten that history per se began in just this way! Herodotus dissolved history in a multiplicity of stories and delightfully simple tales. Yet within these reduced dimensions he was capable of apprehending the human drama—an accomplishment that seems quite beyond the powers of most historians today. The latter are left with only the dry dust of scattered facts—*disjecta membra*—from what once was living reality. In the historical novels of a Sir Walter Scott, a Dumas, or a Galdós a point of view is presented that is totally inadequate—and yet it is at least a partial point of view, one that does allow us to see and understand something of historical reality in a haphazard fashion. We see the intrusion of the historical reality of an era into the private lives of the characters; the era is revealed by the effects it produces on them, like luminous rays striking a screen.

Toward the end of the nineteenth century and in the first decades of the twentieth, some historians, aware that history cannot be written in this way, hit on the promising idea of morphology. This represents an enormous advance, and for the first time history begins to deserve the name. Morphology does, in fact, construct a profile of life. However, it pretends to find in life a static and, in principle at least, a single situation. This is a contradiction, for any situation is dynamically forged from the internal tension of working forces. Morphology really does demonstrate that life had a certain form at a given moment of time, but it does not tell us from whence it came or whither it was going; it does not say *why* it had this form or for what purpose it came into being. In other words, it is unaware of the function of each of the ingredients in a human drama that, in the last analysis, it fails to grasp. And of course, it does not lead us to an understanding of *why* history is dynamic, *why* humanity does not remain forever fixed in this or that historical form; *it does not explain why this could not be.* This weakness is evident even in the most outstanding historical works of the last thirty years, affecting even such men as Huizinga and Paul Hazard. They assume as fact that men lived in a certain way in Flanders and in France in the fourteenth and fifteenth centuries, or in Europe from 1680 to 1715 and in the decades following, and these forms of life *are* marvelously described. Furthermore, the stages in the variation of this kind of life are told; that is, they describe various intermediate forms through which these historical units passed. The missing element in this kind of history is variation itself—in the strictest sense, indeed, history itself.

What is the appearance of a period when we interpret it through generational sequences? Visualize the following.

First, if we take a date for consideration, it immediately begins to unfold before us. We see in it several human strata, coexisting, interacting, each of them with a very precise function. These strata are the generations, specifically four in number:

Generation A—the "survivors" of previous periods without

full historical parts to play anymore but remaining as "geological evidence," as it were, pointing unequivocally to the origin of the present situation;

Generation B—those in power, whose aims correspond in general to the prevailing world style;

Generation C—the "opposition," fully assertive on the historical scene but still lacking leadership powers, struggles against the ruling generation and tries to replace it in authority so as to be able to bring about the changes it feels called upon to champion; and

Generation D—youth, which begins a new life feeling and anticipates the eventual overturn of the present situation: if the older men are the *terminus a quo,* the very young are the *terminus ad quem.*[1]

Plurality and dynamism are readily discernible, then, in a moment of time that at first glance appeared to be a static slice out of the historical flow. The year 1800 is not a single date; it is four different dates that exist simultaneously and are mutually involved in an active form. Strictly speaking, what we find is not movement so much as it is that which shapes movement and makes it possible—a system of tensions and working forces. Movement, in history, cannot be interspersed with periods of inertia, for it arises from the internal tension, the fundamental instability, of any historical situation.

This tension, which is revealed in the multiplicity of genera-

1. The greater incidence of longevity and especially the increase in the average life span have had a double consequence in this century: first, representatives of a time prior to what I call generation A survive in goodly numbers and vigor; second, and more important, these survivors are not only more numerous than before but also more active. If this fact is confirmed and stressed, we may be obliged to consider five generations rather than the usual four, and to alter the sociohistorical function of the second generation accordingly.

tions, is the force behind historical movement. From the outset, leaving aside Generation A, the "survivors" whose function is more subtle but outside of history *sensu stricto,* the theory of generations triples any historical event. This threefold action happens in the case of every historical subject, which is to say in the case of every generation. Rather than accepting an event as a brute and abstract fact, we see the event from *within* history, reverberating in individual lives in different ways according to their generation. A single event appears as an impact on a spectrum of collective life, as a component affecting the entire structure, and with a different function at each level. The "same" historical fact can, then, darken the horizon of Generation D, the young, or facilitate the triumph and dominance of Generation C, the generation of "opposition."

Generations determine the relationships between historical changes. Systems of *vigencias* are replaced by others. The generations, in turn, change their historical role every fifteen years. As the curtain rises on a new fifteen-year period what, we might ask, has happened on the stage? Some actors have disappeared, others have advanced to the footlights, perhaps a new actor appears to play an unfamiliar role. Generation A has disappeared and Generation B has taken over its functions. Generation C, which was preparing to replace Generation B, has done so and is now dominant in all walks of life. Generation D, still obscure fifteen years before, has now taken on a precise role and image and is struggling to make itself heard. A new group, Generation E, is beginning to make its way onto the stage of history. Now, each of these generations will live and experience in a different way the beliefs, ideas, desires, and aims of the period. And each belief, idea, desire, and aim will be a part of the past or the future, a promise or a hope, a limitation or a disappointment, depending on the person and whether he looks backward or to what is yet to come.

It is a matter of seeing history from within, even as it is being created. Since generations are true to the very structure of historical reality, they permit us to reconstruct and relive it, and thus to understand it. Without generations, history is incomprehensible. Who or what are the primary subjects of historical events? individuals? vague indeterminate "peoples"? No, the subjects of historical happenings are the generations.

We have come back to the questions with which we began this book. Who are the characters, we asked, who the "players" of history? What are their ages? What forms the simple "now" of history? Now we see the historical "players" to be generations whose "acts" last fifteen years each. In a dual sense—as a social body and as a temporal duration—a generation is both the cast of characters and the simple "now" in the drama of history.

Once we have established the scale of generations and their effective relationship to each other, history acquires a precise trajectory. We then are able to enter into it and to explain it. The theory of generations thus becomes one of the principal instruments of the historical reason that made the theory itself possible.

This would apparently afford us the opportune moment to commence systematically applying the generational method, or if you like, to begin actually writing history. Were we to do so, we should continue to perfect the method, for as we have seen, the method rectifies itself in its application to empirical reality. However, we shall not determine here the actual sequence of generations. Such an investigation is beyond the limited scope of this book. Hence, we cannot now determine the various generations to which we may belong. On one occasion, without giving the reasons—although he stated they were not few or capricious —Ortega advanced the hypothesis that a certain generation of the last century had the year 1857 as its central point. Following this scale, he spoke occasionally of the Romantic generations and of those of our century. I should be more inclined to fix the date at 1856 and to change the dates of succeeding generations accordingly.[2] The series from the beginning of the nineteenth century would then run: 1811, 1826, 1841, 1856, 1871, 1886, 1901, 1916, 1931, 1946. In any case, this is merely a working hypothesis, useful as a heuristic principle or as a starting point for a thorough and systematic investigation, but for nothing else.

Yet there are several signs that seem to lend some validity to the scale. Remember that 1917 was the year of both the Russian Revolution and the date of the first intervention in European life by the United States. It was also the year that Fascism began to germinate. Approximately fifteen years later, in the first days of 1933, National Socialism triumphed in Germany. Still, great historical events, wars, revolutions, and so on, do not determine generations. They are simply happenings that by their magnitude point to a change of *vigencias,* and this is how I was interpreting them. But these events were not the only indices of change: if we look at the deeper levels of collective life we can see, as a single example, that socially, in about 1917, respect for human life was lost in Eastern Europe. The feeling for life is characteristic, in one of the deepest ways possible, of the different periods. In Western Europe the same loss occurred about fifteen years later. Many can still recall the profound commotion aroused until a short time ago by imposition of the death penalty or an attempt on a person's life: it was as if a shiver ran through the entire social body, as if it collectively felt a violent revulsion more basic than any concern for motives, consequences, justice or injustice. We may recall the events in Spanish politics in 1930, the absence of violence in 1931, the public resistance to the serious penalties that were imposed following the uprisings of 1932. By 1934, however, the climate had changed considerably and public feel-

2. See my article, "La generación de 1856" in *El oficio del pensamiento* (*Obras,* Vol. V).

ing was quite different. After 1936 the new situation led to unexpected extremes. Outside of Spain, the course of events is similar. After 1933 sporadic violence in Germany became frequent. The summer of 1934 saw the first notorious bloody outbreak. In other countries, social pressures delayed violence for several years. But if we look closely, we see that violence was brewing in the minds of people even at this time. Some time ago, as I was completing an *Outline of Our Situation,* I spoke of the cardinal fact of what could be called "the vocation of our time for execution and assassination."[3] This atrocious vocation seems to have been developed around 1931 or 1932 and has now dominated an entire generation. If the hypothesis I have been postulating is true, it must have ended around 1946. Perhaps now we can begin to have hope.

3. Marías, *Introducción a la Filosofía* (*Obras,* Vol. I, 21).

Appendix 1

GENERATIONS IN FRIEDRICH VON SCHLEGEL

In 1949, when I offered a course at the Institute of Humanities in Madrid called "El método histórico de las generaciones" (published in June of that year under the same title), I was obliged to point out several errors—serious, slight, and minute—that had crept into studies of the generations theme with such frequency that one almost had to suspect they were deliberate. After so long a time, the errors are still so frequent, our path still so strewn with stones many times carefully removed, that in preparing a revised edition of the book, I have had to renounce the idea of bringing it "up to date" in other respects, save for a few bibliographical addenda. Even so, some good had to come out of it and it did in the form of a friendly "counteroffensive" by Dámaso Alonso. Three years after publishing my book, I received one of his *Poetas españoles contemporáneos* [Contemporary Spanish Poets] bearing the dedication: "To Julián Marías—pardon the modest attack and be assured of my admiration and affection. Dámaso Alonso." In a note on pages 171–72 appended to the article "A Poetic Generation (1920–1936)," to which I had raised an objection in a comment on it, the "modest attack" is found. It started a merry chase.

Dámaso Alonso writes: "It is curious that Marías, who usually goes at such a careful pace, has failed to consider Friedrich von Schlegel. If Marías had read Harold Stein Jantz' article 'Herder, Goethe and Friedrich Schlegel on the Problem of the Generations,' *Germanic Review*, 1933, vol. 8, pp. 210–38, he would have proceeded with more caution. In his Vienna Lectures of 1812, published three years later under the title *Geschichte der alten und neuen Literatur* [History of Ancient and Modern Literature], Schlegel systematically applied a division of three generations to German literature of the second half of the eighteenth century. This application of a generational method is quite better, believes

Jantz, than any that were to follow in the next hundred years. Furthermore, Schlegel hits on this practice as the result of a theory exactly and compactly expressed. The paragraphs quoted by Jantz can leave no doubt of this."

One can imagine my interest in exploring the path pointed out by Dámaso Alonso. At the same time, for rather complex reasons, I was puzzled that Schlegel should have shown such perfection in his theory. I had not seen Jantz' article, and it required some effort to lay my hands on it. In fact, the difficulty was such that I did something perhaps still more interesting: I read Schlegel's book. If Dámaso Alonso had read it, very likely he would have had some doubt about the theoretical importance of applying the idea of generation to literature, despite the attractiveness of such a procedure. I took advantage of the facilities of the library at the University of Geneva to read *Geschichte der alten und neuen Literatur,* and copied down the passages most interesting from the standpoint of generations.[1] I discovered then there was no need even to look for the text in German, since a Spanish translation of 1843 is available.[2] This work in Spanish is rarely quoted and I think largely unknown.[3] I shall use it here, referring to the German version only for passages of especial importance.

In many instances Schlegel uses the term *generation* in its usual sense and without special stress. For example, in speaking of

1. Friedrich von Schlegel, *Geschichte der alten und neuen Literatur.* Lectures held in Vienna in 1812 (Vienna, 1815).

2. *Historia de la literatura antigua y moderna* (Translation of Schlegel's work into Spanish by P. C., 2 Vols., Barcelona: Librería de J. Olivares y Gavarró, calle de Escudellers; and in Madrid: Librería de Cuesta, calle Mayor [1843]), printed in Barcelona. Hereinafter cited as *Historia.*

3. It is surprising to note the lack of references to this translation in books that, by their subjects, would seem to demand recognition of it. Francisco de Paula Canalejas refers to it rather haphazardly in his *Curso de literatura general* (Madrid, 1868). Menéndez Pelayo also mentions it in *Historia de las ideas estéticas.* Edición Nacional (1940), Vol. 4, p. 147.

Sophocles, he refers to Euripides as "already belonging to a new generation."[4] Likewise, he writes: "Of all the other poets of the first generation, Gessner is the most original."[5] Shortly thereafter, Schlegel becomes more precise: "The example of a writer of this time who seems so deserving of envy, so distinguished, and who really thought he was, shows how relative is the opinion of an age, at least with respect to our literature. . . . It is true," he continues, "that the German writers of the first generation set about in the most laudable way to purify the language. . . ."[6] A few lines further on for the first time he takes up the subject of literature considered from the standpoint of generations, using generations as a principle of division and connection:

> Another division of German literature suggests itself that would offer more results, were this literature considered from a historical point of view during the period from 1750 to 1800. It is quite easy to distinguish precisely the different generations of writers. And it is all the more important to understand this difference since each of these generations exhibits certain characteristic advantages and defects arising from external relationships and the spirit of the time. This point deserves our utmost attention so that we do not demand of a writer qualities that the circumstances of his time prevent him from having, and so that we do not criticize him for shortcomings that belong less to him than to the era.
>
> I group in the first generation those writers whose development and initial efforts begin in the years from 1750 onward till 1770. I have already presented a picture of the more notable poets of this generation. But the limitations of this work do not allow me to name all those deserving mention in this genre. . . .
>
> To this first generation belong, along with the prose writers,

4. Schlegel, *Historia,* Vol. 1, p. 52. Page numbers correspond here and in subsequent notes to the Spanish translation of Schlegel's work.
5. Ibid., Vol. 2, p. 262.
6. Ibid., Vol. 2, p. 270.

several philosphers whom I shall later name, including Kant himself, keeping in mind the date of their birth, the period of their intellectual development, and their first literary attempts. In particular, we could include in this group Lessing and Winckelmann. Chronologically speaking, Hamann also belongs here, but his premonitory depth and foresight mark him as a solitary figure in literature and in his century. . . .

In general the writers of this first generation still displayed many holdovers from the unfavorable situation of German art and language in that period. . . .

Because of their seriousness of purpose and the high aims to which they directed their efforts, the most distinguished writers of this first generation have come to be, properly speaking, the founders of our new German literature.[7]

This is the generations theme introduced in Schlegel's book. The application continues in the following lesson (Chapter 16), where he tries to determine the profile and characteristics of what he calls the second and third generation:

I have tried to trace the picture of the most outstanding poets of the first generation. . . .

We should not be surprised, then, if we see the second generation of German poets and writers, whose first intellectual progress falls largely in the period from 1770–1780, take a much more daring stand and move with infinitely more ease.

7. Ibid., Vol. 2, pp. 270–74. The paragraph in which Schlegel formulates this methodic point of view reads as follows in the original: "Es bietet sich eine andere Eintheilung dar, für die deutsche Literatur, die sich als fruchtbarer bewähren dürfte. Sobald man dieselbe in dem genannten, unstreitig sehr fruchtbaren Zeitraume von 1750–1800 geschichtlich betrachtet, so kann man allerdings die verschiedenen Generationen von Schriftstellern sehr deutlich unterscheiden. Diesen Unterschied aufzufassen ist um so wichtiger, da eine jede von diesen Generationen ihre eigenthümlichen Vorzüge und Mängel hat, wovon der Grund, meistens in den äussern Verhältnisse und in der Zeit selbst lag" (*Geschichte,* Vol. 2, pp. 270–71).

They have harvested and used what their predecessors had sown. Goethe, Stolberg, Voss, and Bürger are poets who characterize this period. In order to persuade ourselves that this period was one of the happiest for the advance of the German spirit, and truly rich in great genius, let us reflect on the fact that Jacobi, Lavater, Herder, and Johann Müller should also be classified with the aforementioned writers, as much because of the date of their writings as their quality. And the glory of these writers has not been restricted to Germany alone, but has spread throughout the rest of Europe. The authors of this second generation differ from those of the first as much in the spirit and structure of their works, as in the language and style. . . .[8]

The third generation of the new German literature differs from the preceding one in a notable and essential way. To have a clear idea of the true character of these later periods and generations of the new German literature, is the surest means of finding the solution to a multitude of bothersome contradictions, and of reconciling many opposing opinions that are based on errors or related to particularities, and are not the result of an essential difference in the way of thinking. The circumstantial setting, the dominant spirit of a period when an author makes his first progress and begins his intellectual development, often sets his character, and at any rate, always exerts a decisive influence on his later career.

I place in the third generation those writers whose appearance and intellectual development date from the last years of the period 1770–1780, or from 1780–1800. The events and prevailing spirit of the time have also undoubtedly exercised here a very notable and important influence on German literature, not only on the writers, but also on the public. . . . If one could characterize with a single word this period as seen from a general view, without fear of being misunderstood, that term would be "revolutionary" . . . The distinctive and characteristic trait of the poets and authors of this third generation is, in my view, that state of mind that leads not only to an external conflict, but also to an inner tension.[9]

8. Ibid., Vol. 2, pp. 276–78.
9. Ibid., pp. 295–97.

194

Schlegel singles out Schiller as an example of this situation. On the other hand he notes:

> The poets and creative writers of the second generation lived their lives with an indifference that seems strange to us. For since that time we have been accustomed to seeing the first symptoms of dangers and revolutions approaching. . . . Instead of this happy indifference in the bosom of the arts, we see the writers of the generation closer to us, those of 1770–1780, or 1780–1800, completely saturated with the spirit of the times, completely under its sway. Either they struggled violently against this spirit, or at least, concentrated in various ways all their energy on it.[10]

Finally, Schlegel turns his gaze toward the future: "I see a new generation being born. It seems to me without doubt that the nineteenth century will assume even in literature a form completely different from that of the eighteenth. Still, the genius and direction of this new generation are not yet sufficiently developed for me to hazard an attempt at defining its character."[11]

These are Schlegel's texts concerning generations. His interest is undeniable, as are his deftness and insight. His works have seldom been used and cited. Henri Peyre referred to them in 1948 (as well as to two articles by Jantz, the one cited by Dámaso Alonso, and "The Factor of Generation in German Literary History," *Modern Language Notes*, May, 1937, vol. 52, pp. 324–30), in his book *Les Générations littéraires* [Literary Generations]. The work contains a wealth of facts and ideas, but it is not without its important omissions and errors, and it is especially lacking in any attempt at a theory or even a concept of generation.[12] But we should now inquire as to the significance of Schlegel's contributions to the theory we have been considering.

At no time does Schlegel even ask what generations are, why

10. Ibid., pp. 298–99.
11. Ibid., p. 318.
12. Henri Peyre, *Les générations littéraires* (Paris, 1948), pp. 72–75. Mention is also made in the bibliography.

there are generations, how long they last, what they include, or how they are determined. There is nothing that could be called a theory of generations, nor even a rigorous concept of generations. He takes his idea of the generation from the commonplace, immemorial notion going back at least to the Old Testament and the *Iliad*. It is the same idea that has been applied countless times to historical reality without any pretense at theory. If we put to Schlegel the questions I have mentioned above, we shall not find the answers anywhere in his works. Up to this point, and until we learn of new examples, we must continue to believe that the first scientific study of generations appears in 1839 in the fourth volume of Comte's *Cours de philosophie positive*.[13] Everything before this, including Schlegel, at best came from a theory that was still far from being formulated. Furthermore, Schlegel's application of the idea is even narrower than Soulavie's, nine years earlier.[14]

On what basis, then, may we consider Schlegel's works to be of interest? Undoubtedly our interest is aroused by the insight he displays in apprehending what we could call the profile of three generations. It was not by chance that Schlegel applied this idea only to his immediate setting: German Literature of the preceding half century. What can be said, and perhaps Jantz did not see this, is that Schlegel saw the generations in a way that we could call "physiognomic." It is especially interesting that in a book on such an imposing theme, a book purporting to examine nothing less than the history of "ancient and modern" literature, it should not occur to Schlegel to make an outline of literature according to generations. He makes not the slightest attempt to establish a general chronology or a pattern of relationships found in the literary past of the different languages. In other words, he does not proceed in the abstract and by principle. Hence there is no theory in his work, not even the hint of a theory, not even a false and misleading theory. Only when he begins to approach his own world, when he can see with his own eyes the literary reality of an

13. See the texts and references in Chapter 2 of this book.
14. See Chapter 2 of this book.

almost contemporary Germany, does this reality appear in the form of generations. It is here that his contribution and his limitation are both to be found. His fine grasp of the *phenomena* of generations is matched only by his lack of a *theory* to explain them. And yet his work would be an excellent starting point for formulating such a theory. What happened is that Schlegel, at least in this book, simply described an example and went no further. The comparison of Schlegel and Dilthey that Jantz offers is not valid. Dilthey's refinements of the idea—in his essay on *Novalis* (1865) and in his inaugural lesson at Basel in 1867, *Die dichterische und philosophische Bewegung in Deutschland 1770–1800* [The Poetic and Philosophical Movement in Germany 1770–1800]—though superior to anything in Schlegel, could be placed on the same plane. But his mature statement of the theme, in *Über das Studium der Geschichte der Wissenschaften vom Menschen, der Gesellschaft und dem Staat 1875* [On the Study of the History of the Science of Man, Society, and the State], is an absolute advance and is irreducible to any "antecedents" that might be found in Schlegel.[15]

A very revealing example of the importance of the notion of generation in Friedrich von Schlegel is the fact that in 1805–1806 he had offered a course in Cologne on "Universal History," in which he attempted to show the divisions and relationships of history. Now then, he does not do this by generations, but by periods, seven in all, from the state of innocence in Paradise (*Stand der Unschuld oder nach unserem System urül teste göttliche Offenbarung* [The Age of Innocence according to Our System of the Oldest Divine Revelation]), to the period corresponding to the Kingdom of God. Furthermore, in 1828 he gave another course in Vienna, "The Philosophy of History," in which he demonstrated a "dividing principle" (*Eintheilungsprinzip*) in history in the form of a "divine impulse." This impulse is manifested historically, and has been the superior principle behind new ways of life for man at every stage of his past.[16] This means that neither

15. For a discussion of Dilthey, see Chapter 2 of this book.
16. See J. H. J. Van der Pot's work, *De Periodisering der Geschiedenis* (The Hague, 1951), pp. 61–62.

before nor after his *History of Ancient and Modern Literature* did it occur to Schlegel to apply the idea of generation to an articulation and interpretation of historical reality.

I believe that these findings place Friedrich von Schlegel's contribution to the generation theme in the proper perspective. He has little to offer to a history of the theory. In a specific case, we find him making a methodical application of the idea to the relationships in literature, but without displaying any precision in his use of the concept. His most worthwhile contribution is what I call the "profile" or "physiognomy" of the three generations immediately preceding his own. Any more charitable evaluation of these works would be misleading. But given the date, 1812, the works turn out to be admirable if we remind ourselves that even today, in the wake of so many theoretical efforts, in the field of literature the notion of generations is often taken simply as it appears in common usage, apart from any theory. When this is done, the life and work of writers close together in time are treated by caprice and without the prudence that Schlegel displayed so long ago. And this is the principal cause of the growing distrust of the generational method, despite its promise, and why this method is being replaced by particular systems based on this or that view, rooted not in an analysis of reality, but in mere unruly impressions.

Appendix 2

GENERATIONS IN IBN KHALDUN

Shall we find it necessary to trace the origin of the theory of generations back to the fourteenth century? Would it be possible? By this I mean, does it strain the imagination to think that at such an early date the necessary groundwork could have been laid so that the theme of generations might appear as a scientific topic? If this were true, we should have to attribute it to genius in the most literal and truest meaning of the term.

Of course, we *are* dealing with genius in this case. Among the many undeniably great minds that have busied themselves with history, one of them is unquestionably Ibn Khaldun. Arabists have long been intrigued by this provocative figure, of course, but even their interest has been less than it should have been. Besides them, the attention paid Ibn Khaldun has been on every hand insufficient. His advent in Western thought occurred with the translation of his principal work in 1862–68 by Baron W. M. de Slane.[1] This French edition has been used in the majority of studies done on him during the following century; among them Ortega's short work, "Ibn Khaldun Reveals the Secret to Us. Thoughts on Africa Minor," written in 1927–28,[2] is notable for its perspicacity and understanding. There is now reason to hope for a revival of interest in Ibn Khaldun among others besides Arabists. Franz Rosenthal, a professor of Semitic languages at Yale, has published an admirable English translation of Ibn Khaldun's most interesting theoretical work, the *Muqaddimah*, which Slane translated as *His-*

---

1. *Prolegomènes historiques d'Ibn Khaldoun*, French translation by William MacGuckin de Slane. Vols. 19–21 of *Notices et extraits des manuscrits de la Bibliothèque Impériale* (Paris, 1862, 1865, 1868).

2. Ortega y Gasset, *Obras*, Vol. 2. pp. 661–79.

torical Prolegomena and which Rosenthal calls *Introduction to History*.[3] The work that went into the Rosenthal translation, with its introductions, notes, and indices, deserves genuine intellectual gratitude. With it we would hope that Ibn Khaldun may now enter directly and forever into the historical and sociological thinking of the West.

Ibn Khaldun was born in Tunis in 1332. He was from a distinguished family of Spanish origin, and lived in various places in the Moslem world, in North Africa, in Spain, in the Near East, and in Cairo, where he died in 1406. He engaged in many activities; he was a politician and held posts in the government; he taught and gave lectures at Islamic universities. In 1377, during a lull in his political duties, he began to write a universal history. It seems that he wrote quite rapidly, although he added to and corrected the manuscript ceaselessly. The part of greatest theoretical interest to us, the introduction, which to some degree is a treatise on historiology or even a kind of incipient sociology when viewed from a different angle, is the writing called *Muqaddimah*. In it arises rather unexpectedly the generations theme.

But is this statement really true? Can we say that in Ibn Khaldun generations are a "theme"? I would say rather that he happens upon the idea of generations, he encounters them in his pathway, as an element with which he must struggle and contend in his history of the Arabic peoples. No, there is nothing that could be called a "theory" of generations in Ibn Khaldun. He deals with them, he discovers them to be an element of reality, as had been done in the Bible, or by Homer and Herodotus. But there is a difference; even without meaning to, almost in spite of himself, he wrests from his materials the shreds of a theory. One could say that while striking a pebble with a steel pick, he causes a spark.

3. Ibn Khaldun, *The Muqaddimah. An Introduction to History*. Translated from the Arabic by Franz Rosenthal. 3 vols., Bollingen Foundation Inc. (New York: Pantheon Books, 1958). Subsequent references are to this work.

This spark was what was on the verge of being the first theory of generations six centuries ago.

When Ibn Khaldun speaks of generations, he is thinking of genealogical generations: forefathers, parents, children, grandchildren, and so on. By no means is he talking of social or historical generations in the strict meaning of these terms. He makes not the slightest reference to the reality of generations, nor to the determining principle of their existence. Nor does it occur to him that history could be structured according to generations. Where then, one might ask, does his importance lie? Why does he deserve to be set apart from those who have held the traditional and ancient notion of genealogical generation? Why is it possible to speak of him as an important forerunner of the theory of generations?

It is the *context* of Ibn Khaldun's notion that gives it an unexpected significance, one that, so far as I know, has not been noted up to now. In the second chapter of his *Muqaddimah* the idea of generation appears in relation to noble families and especially to dynasties. Ibn Khaldun treats the origin and decline of all things, minerals, plants, animals, men, and other created things. Everything is born, grows, declines, and perishes. In this context, the penetrating eye of Ibn Khaldun spots "an accident that affects human beings": "prestige." It follows an inevitable pattern of origin and decline. No man comes from a noble lineage uninterrupted since Adam, except for the Prophet by a special act of grace. Nobility and prestige originate in a state "outside" of leadership and nobility; the conditions of its beginnings are lowly and lacking in prestige. This means that nobility and prestige are preceded by their nonexistence; they can be traced back to a point of origin but no further. Seeking to understand how this process of genesis and decadence works, Ibn Khaldun turns to the generations of men. What is the significance of his so doing?

I consider it to be a sign of his genius as a historian and sociologist. His idea of the generation, I repeat, is simply biological and genealogical; it is the relationship between forebears and descendants. But in relating the idea to prestige, which is a *social* reality, he removes it from biology and genealogy and bestows on

it a historical and social function. We could even say that in trans-
planting the idea of generation to another field, he inadvertently
discovers its true role, and comes ever so close to stating the notion
of *"vigencia."* In a social context—the arena in which prestige
originates and perishes—genealogical generations assume their
real properties, those that only belong to social generations in the
strict sense. Prestige, says Ibn Khaldun, comes to an end in a single
family within the limits of four consecutive generations. He outlines the process as follows: (1) the builder or founder of the
family's glory knows the effort it took to create it; he preserves the
qualities that created and maintained the family's position. (2)
The son who succeeds him has personal contact with his father,
learning these things also. Yet, observes Ibn Khaldun, he is inferior
to his father inasmuch as he who learns through study is inferior to
a person taught by practical experience. (3) The third generation
must content itself with imitating its forebears, and, in particular,
in resting on tradition. This family member is inferior to the second generation, since he who trusts blindly in tradition is inferior
to a person who exercises his own judgment.[4] This astute generalization could be expanded beyond family lineage and applied
to social generations. But Ibn Khaldun does not stop here. (4)
The fourth generation, he goes on to say, is inferior to the preceding in all respects. This member of the family has lost the qualities
that preserved the edifice of its glory; in fact, he comes to scorn
these qualities. *He imagines that the edifice was not built with
solicitude and effort.* He believes it to be something inherent from
the beginning, based on the mere fact of his family's noble birth-
right, and not something that resulted from the efforts of the
family and from individual qualities.[5] Ibn Khaldun traces a picture of the "heir," and at times he resembles the pampered scion
or mass-man, with the psychology of the "spoiled child," described
by Ortega.

The heir sees the respect people have for him but has no idea of

4. *The Muqaddimah,* vol. 1, 279.
5. Ibid., pp. 279–80.

the origin or the reason for it. He believes it a recognition of his "natural" superiority and nothing else. He thinks himself better than others and takes their obedience for granted, without knowing the conditions which this requires. He considers other men contemptible and they, in turn, come to despise him. Finally they rebel and transfer their allegiance to another branch of the family, whose leader has the desired qualities. Accordingly, one family declines and another ascends, assuring a new line of prestige.[6]

This generational process of rise and fall usually involves four generations and forms the complete cycle of prestige. There are four functions, four rôles, one for each of the generations. Ibn Khaldun notes that examples exist of families falling and disappearing before four generations have passed, and others that continue on to the fifth or sixth generation in a state of decadence. He is fully aware that he is dealing with certain rôles; on occasion he describes the generation in other "functional" terms: for instance, the "builder," the one in "personal contact" with the builder, the "believer" in tradition, and the "destroyer." He adds, categorically, that there cannot be fewer elements than these four.[7]

Ibn Khaldun finds the proof for this normal duration of prestige in references to generations in the Koran and the Bible. For instance, when we find the statement, "the noble son of the noble father of the noble grandfather of the noble great-grandfather: Joseph, son of Jacob, son of Isaac, son of Abraham," this means that Joseph had reached the limit of glory. When in Exodus we find that God punishes the sins of the fathers in the children even unto the third or fourth generation, it can be seen that this is the maximum length of time for ancestral prestige to endure in a family. Ibn Khaldun also finds proof for this idea in Muslim history, and he concludes with this observation: "all this shows that prestige lasts only four generations in the best of cases. And God knows best."[8]

6. Ibid., p. 280.
7. Ibid., pp. 280–81.
8. Ibid., pp. 281–82.

In the third chapter of his *Muqaddimah,* Ibn Khaldun turns anew to the theme of generations, but does so from a slightly different point of view that sheds new light on his interpretation. He continues to hold to the genealogical idea and is thus tied to the relationship between parents and children. However, as he begins to stress the fate of dynasties, his interest in collective forms of life compensates somewhat for the merely individual point of departure. In other words, as he delves into the evolution of attitude in successive generations, he passes imperceptibly *from* the personal relationship of each person to his forefathers *to* the way in which a social group (at least the ruling minority of a group) confronts the *vigencias* of their ancestors.

Looking at history with the eyes of a Bedouin, Ibn Khaldun sees in it a process of *refinement.* People become accustomed to having and needing many things. From the mere necessities of life and an austere existence, they pass to luxury, comfort, and beauty; they crave rich food, dress, rugs, and furniture. Each generation wants to outdo the one preceding. Idleness is preferred to activity; cities are built and baths are installed. It is the eternal history of the Arabic peoples: as they become urbanized, they forget the rigorous life of the desert and increasingly abandon themselves to sensuality, comfort, beauty, and art.

Naturally this takes money. Taxes are increased and the people become impoverished. The army has to be reduced and military defense weakened. Furthermore, luxury corrupts the moral fiber; good qualities are lost and evil ones acquired. The dynasty shows signs of dissolution and disintegration, it grows senile, and finally it perishes.

The conclusion drawn from the preceding—and here for the first time a time factor appears in Ibn Khaldun's idea—is that dynasties, like individuals, last for a certain period of time which seems to be granted them by nature. The natural life of individuals, according to Ibn Khaldun, is a hundred and twenty years, what astrologers call the great lunar year.[9] Actually life can be more—or

9. Ibid., p. 343.

probably less. Ibn Khaldun says that a Muslim's life is from sixty to seventy years.

The same thing happens with dynasties. As a general rule, no dynasty endures beyond the life of three generations. Here the reasoning of Ibn Khaldun is not very clear or coherent. He gives forty years as the average duration of a generation, explaining that this is "the life span of a single individual, the time required for him to complete his development and reach maturity."[10] He goes on to say that the lifetime of an individual is identical to that of a generation. Is Ibn Khaldun referring to an *average* longevity? Or is this figure considered to be the time it takes for life to be fully formed, that is, for it to reach full maturity?

Whatever his meaning on that point, Ibn Khaldun is especially interested in describing the features of the succeeding generations. The first generation in a dynasty retains the desert qualities: toughness and savage character. Its members are used to privation and to sharing their glory with one another. They are courageous and rapacious, cunning and feared. The people submit to them. The second generation changes in attitude from that of the desert to a sedentary life, from privation to luxury and abundance, from sharing glory to keeping it for oneself if others are too indolent to seek it, and from haughty superiority to humble servility. The vigor of their spirit is weakened. Nevertheless, many of the old virtues remain, because these men have been in personal contact with the first generation and they have known their qualities. They have lost much, but not everything. They believe former times will return or they cultivate the illusion that conditions have not changed. The third generation, however, has forgotten completely the desert life and its severity. It is as though it had never existed. They have lost their taste for the sweetness of fame and for the group. They go to extremes in luxury and live in riches and ease. They do not know how to defend themselves and must have others do it for them. And so, in the course of just three generations, the dynasty has become senile and exhausted. In the fourth generation prestige

10. Ibid., pp. 343–44.

disappears completely. Three generations last for a hundred and twenty years, and this is the normal lifetime of dynasties.[11]

We see, then, and not without surprise, how the context and the penetrating view of Ibn Khaldun cause a simple genealogical idea of generation actually to "function" as an elementary theory of generations. This is the same more or less trivial view of generation that has existed in history for thousands of years without producing any theoretical offshoot. By exaggerating a bit perhaps, we could say that Ibn Khaldun had no real idea of what generations are. And yet he *did* understand their function. And it is the function that reveals and announces the real nature of a generation.

This early forerunner of the generations theory holds an interest that is readily apparent without need of exaggeration. It forms an intermediate step between the ancient notion derived from life experience and the scientific theorizing of the nineteenth century and since. Between the Bible, Homer, and Herodotus on the one hand, and Comte and his followers on the other, we find this extraordinary Arab who, by himself alone, represents a significant stage of the theory: the historiographical *use* of generations. And he does this without having a theory of generations and without even knowing their nature!

This reference by Ibn Khaldun to the generations could not escape Ortega's notice, and he mentions him in his essay, cited above.[12] But it is surprising that he does so only in passing, and is more interested in what Ibn Khaldun thinks of history than in what he does with this device. What Ortega says includes no suggestion that in the great Tunisian's book there is to be found a concept so rich and full of meaning, revealing such a degree of perception, that it stands out as something completely unexpected and surprising in the work.

I should add that for me personally, the work is everything I have described it to be. Because this *function* or role of generations that Ibn Khaldun discovers in individual and dynastic life seems

11. Ibid., pp. 344–46.
12. Ortega y Gasset, *Obras*, II, pp. 665; 669–71.

to me to be the anticipation of what I observed years ago and which led me to formulate a theory of what I called the "elemental or minimal period" in history. This is the shortest period of time that can constitute a *historical* period, that is, a peculiar form of collective life. To quote from my work *La estructura social* [The Social Structure]:

> The principle of an era or period is never formal or structural, as is that of a generation, but is rather empirical and based on the content of that time period. An elemental period is determined by the appearance within it of "something"—leaving aside for the moment what that "something" might be—characterized by its ability to give a new appearance to life. Now then, if this new life style actually occurs, if a new historical period comes into being, it must needs do so by a historical process in which several generations participate, each with a different rôle. This determines analytically and theoretically the limits of what we could call a "minimal period" or, if you prefer, an "elemental period."
>
> This new "something," which by its presence sets the style of the period, first springs into existence at a given moment as an element in the life aim of a generation. Now, this generation will attempt to impose on the world a view of life shaped by this "something." When the generation has completed its phase of preparation and begins the period of its assertion, that is, when it comes to power after some fifteen years, it will leave for the following generation this "something" already in existence. The men of the following generation are heirs to something that in a strict sense is not theirs; they did not create it. They simply begin to repeat and modify it. This "something," which began as a peculiarity of a minority and which only reached a limited predominance with the maturity of the first generation, is now completely dominant. But this predominance in its complete manifestation is encountered only by the third generation. Its world is predetermined by this "something." This is the "inheriting" generation, the first born in the world of the period in question, that is, born after the period is completely established. This situation—*mutatis mutandis*—may be repeated. A whole series of generations may live under the shelter of a particular

world form that continues to prevail, although the succeeding generations may each effect alterations. But it may happen also, in the case of the "minimal period," that the *vigencia* of this world form weakens with the fourth generation. It is possible for the fourth generation to live within a world defined by the "something" that has been the guiding principle of an entire period, yet the collective aspiration of this generation no longer finds expression in this world view. In this case, the "world" of this generation is still affected by the older view, but for the fourth generation that view is simply something inherited and inert, and which it does not really feel. The social behavior of each man is conditioned by this inherited factor but his private aim is different. There occurs, then, in this generation the crisis of the period and the transition, at least the first steps, toward another period.[13]

It seems to me that our inquiry into Ibn Khaldun's work shows, better than any other line of reasoning, the grand sweep of what he glimpsed in 1377 or thereabouts. The pages of his work have revealed many secrets and doubtless contain many more yet to be discovered.

13. Marías, *La estructura social, Obras,* II, p. 9.

Bibliography

THE LIST OF BIBLIOGRAPHICAL REFERENCES OFFERED HERE IS not exhaustive by any means. Nor do I claim that every important author or work on the problem of generations is included. If I offer certain references, I do so for the reader's convenience and not as a display of mere erudition for its own sake. The works that are of the greatest interest for history and the theory of generations, in my judgment, are marked by an asterisk. For those writers who have treated the topic in several works, I cite only the principal titles. Pre-nineteenth century works have been omitted.

*Abenjaldún (Ibn Khaldun). *The Muqaddimah. An Introduction to History*. Translated by Franz Rosenthal. New York: Pantheon Books, 1958.

Agathon (Alfred Tarde, Henri Massis). *Les jeunes gens d'aujourd'hui*. Paris: Plon-Nourrit, 1913.

Ageorges, Joseph. *La marche montante d'une génération (1890–1910)*. Paris, 1912.

Alewyn, Richard. "Das Generationsproblem in der Geschichte," *Zeitschrift für deutsche Bildung* (1929).

Alonso, Dámaso. "Una generación poética (1920–1936)," *Finisterre*, tome I, fasc. 3 (March, 1948).

Aly, Wolf. *Geschichte der griechischen Literatur*. Leipzig: Bielefeld, 1925.

*Ayala, Francisco. *Tratado de Sociología*. Vol. 2 of *Sistema de la Sociología*. Buenos Aires: Editorial Losada, 1947.

Azorín (José Martínez Ruiz). "La generación del 98," *Clásicos y modernos*. Salamanca: Ediciones Anaya, 1961.

Bainville, Jacques. *Histoire de trois générations, 1815–1918*. Paris: Nouvelle Librairie Nationale, 1918.

Baroja, Pío. "Tres generaciones." 1926 (lecture).

*Benloew, Louis. *Les lois de l'histoire*. Paris: Germer-Baillière, 1881.

Bernheim. *Lehrbuch der historischen Methode*. Leipzig: Verlag von Duncker und Humbolt, 1889.

Boll, Franz Johanes. *Die Lebensalter. Ein Beitrag zur antiken Ethologie und zur Geschichte der Zahlen*. Berlin: B. G. Tuebner, 1913.

Brinckmann, A. E. *Spätwerke grosse Meister*. Frankfurt am Main: Frankfurter Verlags-Anstatt a. g., 1925.

Bula Piriz, Roberto. *Antonio Machado*. Montevideo: 1954.

Carilla, Emilio. *Literatura argentina 1800–1950 (Esquema generacional)*. Tucumán: 1954.

Caturla, María Luisa. *Arte de épocas inciertas*. Madrid: Revista de Occidente, 1944.

*Ceplecha, Christian, O. S. B. *The Historical Thought of José Ortega y Gasset*. Washington, D. C.: Catholic University of America Press, 1958.

*Comte, Auguste. *Cours de philosophie positive*. Paris: J. B. Baillière, 1864.

*———. *Système de politique positive*. Paris: La Société Positiviste, 1929.

*Cournot, Antoine-Augustin. *Considérations sur la marche des idées et des événements dans les temps modernes*. Paris: Hachette, 1872.

Croce, Benedetto. *History and its Theory and Practice*. Translated by Dougles Amslie. New York: Russell and Russell, 1960.

———. *Teoria e storia della storiografia*. Bari: 1920.

Curtius, E. R. *Die literischen Wegbereiter des neuen Frankreichs*. Potsdam: G. Kiepenheuer, 1920.

Díaz-Plaja, Guillermo. *Modernismo frente a noventa y ocho*. Madrid: Espasa Calpe, 1951.

*Dilthey, Wilhelm. *Das Leben Schleiermachers*. 1870.

210

————. *Die dichterische und philosophische Bewegung in Deutschland 1770–1800*. 1867.

————. *Novalis*. 1865.

————. *Über des Studium der Geschichte der Wissenschaften vom Menschen, der Gesellschaft und dem Staat*. 1875.

*Drerup, Engelbert. *Das Generationsproblem in der griechischen und griechischrömischen Kultur*. Paderborn: F. Schöningh, 1933.

*Dromel, Justin (Écorcheville). *La loi des révolutions. Les générations, les nationalités, les dynasties, les religions*. Paris: Didier, 1862.

Durkheim, Emile. *De la division du travail social*. Paris: F. Alcan, 1893.

Écorcheville. [See: Dromel.]

Eisenstadt, S. N. *From Generation to Generation. Age Groups and Social Structure*. Glencoe, Illinois: Free Press, 1956.

Escarpit, Robert. *Sociologie de la littérature*. Paris: Presse Universitaire de France, 1958.

Fernández, María Ángela. *Un lapso en la historia del pensamiento y de la cultura argentinos, 1820–1880*. Buenos Aires: 1938.

Fernández Méndez, Eugenio. "Criterios de la periodización cultural de la historia," *Cuadernos del Seminario de problemas científicos y filosóficos*, National University of Mexico (1959).

Fernández Moreno, César. "La cuestión de las generaciones," *El 40*, Buenos Aires (1952).

Ferrari, Giuseppe. *Corso sugli scrittori politici italiani*. Milan: 1862.

————. *Filosofia della Rivoluzione*. 2 vols. London: 1851.

————. *Histoire de la raison d'État*. Paris: Michel Lévy Frères, 1860.

————. *Histoire des révolutions d'Italie*. Paris: Didier, 1858.

————. *La Chine et l'Europe, leur histoire et leurs traditions comparées*. Paris: Didier, 1867.

————. *Philosophie de la révolution*. Paris: 1851.

————. *Teoria dei periodi politici*. Milan: V. Hoepli, 1874.

Ferrater Mora, José. *Diccionario de Filosofía*. Buenos Aires: Editorial Sudamericana, 1958.

Freyre, Gilberto. *Ordem e Progresso*. (Preface). Río de Janeiro: J. Olympío, 1959.

Gaos, José. "Sobre sociedad e historia," *Filosofía de la filosofía e historia de la filosofía*. Mexico: 1947.

Giraud, V. *Les maîtres de l'heure*. Paris: Librairie Hachette, 1914.

González Freire, Natividad. *Teatro cubano contemporáneo (1928–1952)*. Havana: 1958.

Grimm, Jacob. *Uber das Alter*. n.d., n.p.

Gründel, Ernst Günther. *Die Sendung der jungen Generation*. Munich: Beck, 1932.

Hamann, Richard. *Die deutsche Malerei vom Rokoko bis zum Expressionismus*. Berlin: B. G. Teubner, 1925.

———. *Die Frührenaissance der italianischen Malerei*. Jena: E. Diederichs, 1909.

Heidegger, Martin. *Sein und Zeit*. Tübingen: M. Niemeyer, 1967.

Honigsheim, P. "Die Pubertät," *Kölner Vierteljahrshefte für Soziologie*, III, 4 (1924).

Hoog, Alemand. "L'Idée de génération," *La Nef*, Paris (1954).

Huizinga, J. "Problemas de historia de la cultura," *El concepto de la historia*. Mexico: 1946.

Ibn Khaldun. [See: Abenjaldún].

Jantz, Harold Stein. "Herder, Goethe and Friedrich Schlegel on the Problem of the Generations," *Germanic Review*, VIII (October, 1933).

———. "The Factor of Generation in German Literary History," *Modern Language Notes* (May, 1937).

Jeschke, Hans. *Die Generation von 1898 in Spanien*. Halle: 1934.

———. *La generación de 1898; ensayo de una determinación de su esencia*. Translated by Y. Pino Saavedra. Madrid: Editora Nacional, 1954.

Joël, K. "Das säkuläre Rhythmus der Geschichte," *Jahrbuch für Soziologie*, Karlsruhe (1925).

———. *Wandlungen der Weltanschauung*. Tübingen, Mohr, 1928–1934.

Kehrer, Ferdinand Adalbert. *Der Wandel der Generationen. Eine biologischsoziologische Studie*. Stuttgart: F. Enke, 1959.

Kummer, F. *Deutsche Literaturgeschichte des 19 Jahrhunderts, dargestellt nach Generationen*. Dresden: G. Reissner, 1922.

Lafuente Ferrari, Enrique. *La fundamentación y los problemas de la historia del arte*. Madrid: Editorial Tecnos, 1951.

*Laín Entralgo, Pedro. *La generación del noventa y ocho*. Madrid: Espasa Calpe, 1963.

212

*Laín Entralgo, Pedro. *Las generaciones en la historia.* Madrid: Instituto de estudios políticos, 1945.

La Lande de Calan, Charles de. "La race et le milieu," *Annales des sciences politiques* (1901).

Littré Émile. *Paroles de philosophie positive.* Paris: A. Delahays, 1860.

Lorenz, A. *Abendländische Musikgeschichte im Rhythmus der Generationen; eine Anrogung.* Berlin: M. Hesse, 1928.

*Lorenz, Ottokar. *Die Geschichtswissenschaft in Hauptrichtungen und Aufgaben kritisch erörtert.* Berlin: W. Hertz, 1886.

*————. *Leopold von Ranke, die Generationslehre und der Geschichtsunterricht.* Berlin: W. Hertz, 1891.

*Mannheim, Karl. "Das Problem der Generationen," *Kölner Vierteljahrshefte für Soziologie,* VII, 2–3 (1928).

Maravall, J. A. "Barroco y racionalismo," *Finisterre* (February, 1948).

Martínez Ruiz, José. [See: Azorín].

Massis, Henri. [See: Agathon].

*Mentré, François. *Les générations sociales.* Paris: Bossard, 1920.

*Mill, John Stuart. *A System of Logic, Ratiocinative and Inductive.* London: Parker, 1862.

Müller, Hans von. *Die namhafteren deutschen Dichter und Denker seit Reimarus und Günther, in Altersgruppen geordnet.* Berlin: M. Breslaver, 1917.

Nohl, H. "Das Verhältnis der Generationen in der Pädagogik," *Die Tat* (May, 1914).

*Ortega y Gasset, José. *El tema de nuestro tiempo.* Madrid: Revista de Occidente, 1923.

*————. *En torno a Galileo.* Madrid: Revista de Occidente, 1933.

*Perriaux, Jaime. *Las generaciones argentinas.* Buenos Aires, 1970.

*Petersen, Julius. *Die Literarischen Generationen.* Berlin: Junker und Dünnhaupt, 1930.

*————. *Die Wesenbestimmung der deutschen Romantik.* Leipzig: Quelle, 1926.

*————. *Die Wissenschaft von der Dichtung I.* Berlin: Junker und Dünnhaupt verlag, 1939.

Petitjean, Armand. "Éléments d'une génération," *Combats préliminaires,* Paris (1942).

*Peyre, Henri. *Les Générations littéraires.* Paris: Boivin, 1948.

213

*Pinder, Wilhelm. *Das Problem der Generation in der Kunstgeschichte Europas*. Berlin: Frankfurter Verlags-Anstalt, 1926.
———. *Kunstgeschichte nach Generationen. Zwischen Philosophie und Kunst. Johannes Volkelt zum 100. Lehrsemester dargebracht.* Leipzig: E. Pfeiffer, 1926.
Platz, Hermann. *Geistige Kämpfe in modernen Frankreich.* München: J. Kösel und F. Pustet, 1922.
Pommier, Jean. "L'Idée de génération," *Questions de critique et d'histoire littéraire.* Droz: 1945.
*Ranke, Leopold. *Geschichten der romanischen und germanischen Völker von 1494 bis 1514 Jahrhundert.* Leipzig: 1884.
*———. "Über die Epochen der neueren Geschichte. Vorträge dem Könige Maximilian II. von Bayern gehalten (1854)," *Weltgeschichte,* IV, Leipzig (1910).
Recasens Siches, Luis. *Lecciones de Sociología.* Mexico: Editorial Porrúa, 1949.
———. *Tratado general de filosofía del derecho.* Mexico: Editorial Porrúa, 1959.
Remos y Rubio. *Historia de la literatura cubana.* Havana: Cárdenas, 1945.
Renouard, Yves. "La notion de génération en histoire," *Revue Historique,* Vol. 209 (January–March, 1953).
Rosenstock-Huessy, Eugen. *The Christian Future, or the Modern Mind Outrun.* New York: C. Scribner's Sons, 1946. (Harper & Row "Torchbook" edition, with Introduction by Harold Stahmer, New York, 1966.)
———. *Out of Revolution: Autobiography of Western Man.* New York: W. Morrow and Co., 1938. (Paperback reprint, with introductory essays by Page Smith et al.)
Rothacker, Erich. *Über die Möglichkeit und den Ertrag einer genetischen Geschichtschreibung im Sinne K. Lamprechts.* Leipzig: R. Voigtländer, 1912.
*Rümelin, Gustav. "Über den Begriff und lie Dauer einer Generation," *Reden und Aufsätze.* Tübingen: 1875.
Sainte-Beuve. [See: Petitjean].
Salazar, Adolfo. *El siglo romántico.* Madrid: 1936.
———. *La música en el siglo XX.* Madrid: 1936.
Salinas, Pedro. "El concepto de generación literaria aplicada a la del 98," *Revista de Occidente,* L (December, 1935).

214

Sánchez, Federico. "El método orteguiano de las generaciones y las leyes objetivas del desarrollo histórico," *Nuestras Ideas,* Brussels (1957).

Scheidt, Walter. *Lebensgesetze der Kultur. Biologische Betrachtungen zum Problem der Generation in der Geistesgeschichte.* Berlin: 1929.

Scherer, Wilhelm. *Geschichte des deutschen Literatur.* Berlin: Weidmann, 1902.

*Schlegel, Friedrich von. *Geschichte der alten und neuen Literature.* Regensburg: J. Habbel, 1911.

Schurtz, H. *Altersklassen und Männerbünde. Eine Darstellung der Grundformen der Gesellschaft.* Berlin: G. Reimer, 1902.

Seillière, Ernest. *Le Romantisme.* Paris: 1925.

――――. *Romanticism.* Translated by Cargill Sprietsma. New York: Columbia University Press, 1929.

Sepúlveda Villanueva, Héctor. "Dos generaciones en la historia. La generación de 1810 y la de Portales." Santiago de Chile, 1951 (Unpublished).

Serrano Poncela, Segundo. "Las generaciones y sus constantes existenciales," *Realidad,* Buenos Aires, VI (July–August, 1949).

*Soulavie, Jean Luis. *Pièces inédites sur les règnes de Louis XIV, Louis XV et Louis XVI.* Paris: L. Collin, 1809.

――――.*Tableaux de l'histoire de la décadence de la monarchie française.* Paris: L. Duprat, 1803.

Spranger, Eduard, *Psychologie des Jugendalters.* Leipzig: Quelle und Meyer, 1931.

Sobrinho, Paulo Cretella, and Strenger, Irineu. *Sociologia das geraçoes.* São Paulo: 1952.

Tarde, Alfred. [See: Agathon].

Valois, Georges: D'un siècle à l'autre, chronique d'une génération. Paris: Nouvelle Librairie Nationale, 1924.

Van der Pot, J. H. J. "De Periodisering der Geschiedenis," *Overzicht der Theoriëen.* The Hague: 1951.

Vogel, Walter. "Über den Rhythmus in geschichtlichen Leben des abendländischen Europa," *Historische Zeitschrift,* Vol. 129 (1924).

*Wechssler, Eduard. "Das Problem der Generationen in der Geistesgeschichte,"*Davoser Revue* (1929).

*――――. *Die Generation als Jugendreihe und ihr Kampf und die Denkform.* Leipzig: Quelle & Meyer, 1930.

Wiese, Leopold von. *Allgemeine Soziologie als Lehre von den Beziehungbedingungen der Menschen.* Munich: Dunker & Humbolt, 1924.

————. "Väter and Söhne," *Der neue Strom,* I, 3.

Wustmann, Rudolf. *Deutsche Geschichte nach Menschenaltern erzählt.* Leipzig: E. A. Seemann, 1911.

Zamora, Alonso. "Sobre petrarquismo." Santiago: 1945 (lecture).

Zeuthen, H. J. "Quelques traits de la propagation in la science de génération en génération," *Rivista di Scienza* (1909).

Index

220